HANDBOOK
of effective church letters

STEWART HARRAL

HANDBOOK
of effective church letters

$\textstyle\oint$ *ABINGDON PRESS   NEW YORK   NASHVILLE*

HANDBOOK OF EFFECTIVE CHURCH LETTERS

Copyright © 1965 by Abingdon Press

Library of Congress Catalog Card Number: 65-15233

SET UP, PRINTED, AND BOUND BY THE
PARTHENON PRESS, AT NASHVILLE,
TENNESSEE, UNITED STATES OF AMERICA

TO MEMBERS OF THE FELLOWSHIP CLASS
*for the spiritual lift they have given me
as teacher for sixteen years*

CONTENTS

CONTENTS

1

HOW TO
multiply yourself

Ever since the time of Paul letters have been used to serve great Christian purposes. Through the centuries countless missionaries, preachers, and other religious leaders have spread the gospel by means of personal messages. But strange as it may seem, most ministers today overlook the power of personalized letters to vitalize and strengthen their public relations program.

With most pastors carrying a heavy load—in counseling, preaching, and administration—more and more of them are gradually finding how sincere letters can ease their load and also move the hearts of men.

As civilization has grown more complex, the transmission of ideas has quickened. As competitive forces have multiplied and expanded, it has become increasingly apparent to church leaders that they must win and hold public approval, if they are to survive in the welter of competing forces struggling for public favor.

As a pastor you have but one choice: To secure the support and understanding of people in this competitive age you must not only have a public relations policy but also a definite public relations program. You must make wise use of all channels of communication—speeches, exhibits, posters, broadcasts, news stories, movies, telecasts, special events, photographs, and others—but you should certainly use more letters to elevate the public's understanding, trust, and appreciation of the church.

Every letter—whether a brief congratulatory note or a detailed message on the coming year's budget—is a public relations letter. Why? Because each letter is a representative of the church. As such it carries a powerful impact.

Effective letters perform a variety of jobs. They can (a) alter a belief or an attitude; (b) interpret a policy, activity, or program; (c) bring harmony into a tense situation; (d) promote stewardship; (e) stimulate attendance; (f) strengthen loyalty; (g) express gratitude and appreciation; (h) make individual contacts with members of a large congregation; (i) keep members informed about needs, achievements, problems; (j) build good will, support, and cooperation; (k) win converts; and (l) strengthen the image of the church.

Perhaps you are saying, "But letters can never substitute for my personal ministry." And you are right. But in many situations they can augment and strengthen your personal contacts. At times a letter is the best way to communicate. And certainly by combining the two methods you can greatly expand the sphere of your influence.

Letters provide you a tested method of maintaining two-way communication between you and your congregation. Your congregation—let's say you have 1,800 members—is a lot of individuals. And the best way of reaching an individual (whether he attends regularly or not) is by letter. No matter where a person lives, you can reach him by letter.

Here's something else: Letters help satisfy a human need. They possess a psychological plus. You know the feeling that comes over you when you have received a real, friendly, human, sincere letter. From childhood to old age you can get a wonderful thrill from a letter.

Of all the tasks that church letters perform, the most important is to represent favorably and ably the whole organization. In short, they are good-will ambassadors. From a public relations viewpoint the church's letters are—or should be— a bulwark of church prestige and influence, an important complement to a church's entire promotion efforts. For this reason alone every pastor must give more emphasis to letters if he hopes to succeed in the spirited battle for people's attention.

Effective church letters are extremely hard to find. Many a church whose program is quite excellent in most areas permits its daily mail to go on a dull routine (if it goes on at all) and ignores the major role that letters play in vitalizing religious activities.

Every letter makes friends for your church—or loses them. Cold, impersonal letters can nullify the friendliness built up by other activities. But when letters are friendly and interesting, persuasive and tactful, telling the good news of the gospel, you can strengthen your public relations impact and bring men and women into the Kingdom.

In this guidebook you will find a collection of tested ideas, devices, and techniques used by successful ministers, noted direct mail experts, public relations correspondence authorities, and letter-writing consultants.

Things like: specific ingredients which make a letter outstanding; how to acquire word magic in messages; ways of capitalizing on complaints; tested methods of getting readers to respond; effective ways of building cooperation, stewardship, and understanding by letter; extras which give letters higher readership; and many others.

Best of all, you will find over two hundred examples of successful letters, used by churches, large and small, which you may adapt "as is" to scores of situations in your church.

Using this book, with its many tested ideas and devices,

11

you'll step up your total impact as a minister. Patterns of successful letters—shown in specific examples—are revealed. You will see how letters can perform a variety of tasks. For the first time you can read and analyze techniques of letter writing successfully used by many noted ministers. Put these ideas to work for you in your parish. You'll develop into a competent letter writer and thus "let your light so shine before men." You can multiply yourself by extending your ministry. Just try it and see.

2

HOW TO
flag the reader's attention

What's the weakest part of most letters?

It's likely to be your beginning, which is not surprising. It is usually more difficult to get a letter started than to keep it going once the forward motion has been induced. Unfortunately there is no spot where weakness could do more harm. Never forget: Your opening sentence may make or break your letter, no matter what is said afterward.

Somehow you must make the first few words—a few fleeting seconds—really count. The more you can woo the reader with words—words that intrigue, that strike bells of attention and pleasantly say "Wake up!" to the reader's mind—the more dramatic your opening.

What should the beginning accomplish? That depends on the kind of letter. "Put the reader in the letter right at the beginning," Sherman Perry tells us in *Let's Write Good Letters*. He continues, "Write something of interest to him. Begin promptly. The beginning paragraph is your point of contact."

How can you get off to a fast start? You must say something interesting—dramatic—compelling—something significant. To uncover the striking feature in a mass of facts and ideas and then weld it into the opening sentence is an art. But you can learn to do this by constant thought, observation, practice, and revision.

Here are a few weak lead-off lines—all of them by persons who shifted into neutral before their brain was in motion:

I believe that every church member, sooner or later, thinks about financial support. . . .

I have before me your letter of February 16, in which you point out. . . .

Your interesting letter, dated October 8, has been received and its contents carefully noted. . . .

In reply to your request of June 10, which reached me this morning, I wish to state that. . . .

Contrast those dull, listless openings with a few that have attention value and animation necessary to stimulate interest:

You and I—and all the other folks who are alive and kicking today—have one big thing in common.

Good-bye.

That's a word I hate to say. For now, after nine years in Middletown, during which Mrs. Hagar and I have been so close to all of you and so happy in our ministry here . . . and suddenly, I have to say "good-bye." Believe me, it isn't easy.

What is the Most Powerful Force to Give Life, Power, and Direction? The one ingredient for giving you a zest and happiness, without which everything else is meaningless?

The answer is TOTAL COMMITMENT.

Will you do me a favor . . .

. . . and take just a few moments to answer any or all of the brief questions on the back of this letter? Your answers are important and will be carefully read and considered.

During the Depression

... 'tis said, one struggling rural church posted this sign on the lawn: "Strawberry Festival Saturday Night but on Account of Hard Times Prunes Will Be Served."

VISUALIZE YOUR READER

Before writing or dictating a single word ask yourself, "Who is my reader? What does he seek in life? What are his basic needs? How can I get in step with him in the first few words? Above all, how can my letter help him to satisfy one of his psychological needs?"

Now that you have identified your reader, remember that your opener must accomplish three things:

1. You must get on common ground—establish rapport—with the reader.
2. It should contain an incentive, a reason why he should read your letter.
3. It should lead the reader logically, smoothly, and easily into the message.

Actually there's no one way to get a letter "off the ground." You may relate your opening to the reader's role in church life. At times you arouse his curiosity. Your letter may amuse him. In some situations you catch his interest by telling a story in much the same way the Master held the attention of his hearers as he gave the parables. Occasionally you can use a question as an opener (it should always be asked so that the remainder of your letter has a chance to do its job—persuade the reader). Now let's look at just a few of the many ways of getting off to a good start:

1. USE A DRAMATIC OPENING

    Yesterday I met with other district superintendents, and I really stuck my neck out.

15

2. PASS ALONG A PIECE OF NEWS
   Have you heard the good news?

3. ASK A FAVOR
   I need your advice.

4. START WITH A STORY OR INCIDENT
   Last week I ran into an unusual problem.

5. STATE AN ACCEPTED FACT
   The worst thing about a budget is that it will not stretch.

6. AROUSE CURIOSITY
   It's impossible—but it happened—last Sunday.

7. USE AN HISTORICAL TIE-IN
   Columbus never did know where he was going, and when he got home he didn't know where he had been. You'll remember, too, that he made the trip on borrowed money.

8. ADD AN AMUSING COMMENTARY
   All of us, at some time or other, are like the churchman who thought the epistles were the wives of the apostles.

9. STATE SOMETHING OF INTEREST TO THE READER
   Certainly, Mr. Finney, we understand your situation.

10. TRY HEADLINE OPENING (often effective in mass mailings)
    ABOUT THE ONLY THING
    that'll give you more for your money now than ten years ago is the penny weight scale at the drug store.

A GENUINE ATHEIST

is a man who goes to the Notre Dame-SMU football game and doesn't cheer.

WHEN YOUR RELIGION

gets into the past tense it becomes pretense.

11. MAKE A COURTEOUS REQUEST

You can help to show 100 per cent participation at the district rally by returning your card before Monday.

12. CHALLENGE THE READER

Will you help me make a dream come true?

13. START WITH A TESTIMONIAL

"The most rewarding vacation we've ever enjoyed."

"Lots of inspiration and fun. Can hardly wait to go again."

"All of us grew spiritually. Lots of fun, fellowship, and food."

—wrote three church members, telling us why they enjoyed our annual Family Camp.

TRY AND THEN TRY AGAIN

Writing openings that are good in a variety of letters is a real chore. Occasionally they just come; they just seem to flow out of a situation. But most of the time they are the result of deliberation, trying and trying again.

Maybe you're asking, "Shall I write the opening first?" Some writers do. Others do better after the body of the letter is written. If it is good, the copy frequently suggests ways to improve the beginning. Here is the main thing: Experiment and revise until you say something worthy of emphasis, something interesting, something easy for the reader to understand at a glance.

17

Your reader will allow you only four or five seconds in which to convince him that your letter is worth reading. Think of your first sentence as the "headline" of your letter. Here is your only opportunity to catch and hold the reader's attention.

Make the beginning interesting but don't try to hoodwink your reader. He doesn't like monkey business. If you start with a ridiculous statement just to lure him into the message, don't be surprised if he tosses the letter into the wastebasket. Glance at the following examples:

Do you want to go to heaven?
Are you helping the church to die spiritually?
Just how quiet is a church mouse?
We haven't any idea, but we couldn't help wondering why your pledge has not been paid.

There is no denying that those openings would irritate any reader. All of them ask questions too ridiculous to be read. Instead of trying to "sneak up on the reader" lead him into the heart of your message as quickly as tact and good psychology will permit.

WRITE FROM THE HEART

Have you ever received a letter which lacked feeling? Oh yes, the words were there, but it lacked a warm, human touch; it lacked friendliness. Perhaps the writer dashed it off fifteen minutes before five o'clock. Or maybe it was a "form letter" which is easy to detect because it is flat and cold. Either type lacks a ring of genuineness and sincerity.

One of the nation's best-known ministers gets an excellent response from his letters. Why? "You've got to believe it before you say it," he explains. "I use the old trick of visualizing my reader across the desk from me, and then I write to him

18

as though we might be visiting. This helps me to stay on a friendly, conversational level."

That's good advice. It's true whether you are writing a letter to Mrs. Herbert Putnam or a message to all three thousand members of your church. And you ask, "How can you personalize a letter used in a mass mailing?" Try this: Think of a typical member. Visualize what makes him or her tick. Pinpoint the person's psychological needs or interests. Then gear your message to one of these basic wants. Obviously the letter used in a mass mailing cannot be custom-made to fit each member of your church. But if you know your congregation well enough—age, sex, education, occupation, social status, income, psychological makeup, and other characteristics—you can write a friendly letter which will bring the desired response.

Keep in mind that today you have access to a tremendous amount of research findings showing what makes people click. Unless you are extremely careful you may rely too much on verbal, logical, direct approaches. "We have been brought up for so long in a physical world that even two thousand years after Christ, and five thousand years after Moses, we still do not truly believe in the power of the mind and the soul," Ernest Dichter says in *The Strategy of Desire*. Mix facts with emotions and you'll catch and hold the reader's attention.

How do you plan your opening? Begin by asking, "What does the reader want to hear? What will interest him? How can I attract and hold his attention? How does he look at life?" Next, jot down every idea that comes to mind—good or bad. Try several versions. Combine one of his interests with your idea. Then from many possibilities pick the best one. Mail your letter and when your reader sees the first sentence and it says, "I'm important—I'm interesting!" he will read on and respond!

3

HOW TO
spotlight Mr. Reader

Just for a moment, think of the most agreeable person you know. Why did you choose him?

The chances are that it's because he is interested in you, your family, your interests, your hobbies, the things you do. Like all well-liked persons, he thinks, acts, and speaks in terms of others' interests.

Benjamin Franklin discovered this a long time ago when he confessed, "I early found that when I worked for myself alone, myself worked along for me; but when I worked also for others, others worked also for me."

"You" is the most powerful word in your language.

"We" is next strongest.

"I" is the smallest and weakest.

In letter writing remember that your reader is more interested in himself than anything else in the world. That's why you must flag his attention and hold it by talking to him in terms of his interests, his hopes, his preferences, his problems, his dreams.

Try this sometime: Read a few carbons of letters which you have written or dictated and then circle each "we" and "I" and "our." In all probability you'll find that you are writing most letters from the first-person angle.

Much has been written in books and magazines about the "you" attitude. And time after time correspondence experts have pointed out the importance of presenting each message from the reader's point of view. But not enough writers have followed this advice. Most of us still cling to the habit (and it's a natural one) of telling our readers what WE want and just what they can do to help us.

Now let's look at several ways of changing "we" and "our" phrases into "you" approaches:

WE-OUR	YOU
Visitors at the church night dinner will hear . . .	You will hear . . .
Our members will understand the reason for this.	You will understand the reason for this.
We are pleased to announce our new nursery hours.	Now you can enjoy the convenience of additional hours.
Ability to use our projector is a "must" in Sunday school teaching today.	As an alert teacher you know how much effective movies can hold the attention of your group.
Never before have we presented such an inspiring evening of gospel songs.	You'll receive a thrill when you hear these old-time gospel songs.
All of our members will find that the new elevator will get them to the sanctuary with comfort and speed.	With the new elevator you can get to the sanctuary with comfort and speed.

No matter how many writing devices you master, you can never get "you" into your letters unless you practice empathy. It's the spirit—a vital necessity—that bridges the chasm between you and your reader. It's the ability to see the world

21

through his glasses, to wear another man's shoes, to peek into the universe where he faces life. It's the handshake in your letter; it's the display of interest in those things, persons, and ideas nearest and dearest to the reader.

As a minister you are deeply interested in people, not as psychological specimens but as persons. Morgan Phelps Noyes says that "no pastoral relationship is possible without that kind of friendly interest." And Ralph W. Sockman in his book *The Highway of God* warns that "a genuine concern cannot long be simulated." "When we convince another that we care for his welfare, we win his interest. To be interested in others is to be interesting to them."

Surprisingly rare is the pastor who can analyze his message and present it in terms of what will interest the recipient. It's easy if you remember this: Don't bore your reader by telling what you want because he feels neglected while you talk about yourself. Instead, appeal to his self-interest—talk about him.

Note the variety of these "you approaches":

1. GET IN STEP WITH YOUR READER; WHENEVER POSSIBLE AGREE WITH HIS THINKING, HIS SUGGESTION, HIS INTENTIONS.

    You are exactly right.

2. SPELL HIS NAME CORRECTLY

3. SHOW THAT YOU APPRECIATE HIS POINT OF VIEW

    You are right—three weeks is indeed a long time to wait for the organ to be repaired and you have a right to be concerned. One of the parts ordered from the factory was missent to New Hampshire, but it came this week and we hope that the organ will be ready by Easter Sunday.

4. USE HIS NAME AT SEVERAL PLACES IN YOUR LETTER

You'll admit, John, that one sure way of getting more substitute Sunday school teachers is to . . .

5. DON'T BEAT AROUND THE BUSH WHEN YOU SHOULD APOLOGIZE

Is my face red?

6. HELP YOUR READER TO "SAVE FACE"

So you think you pulled a boner? But listen to what happened to me one day.

7. GIVE HIM CREDIT FOR UNDERSTANDING THE NATURE OF THE PROBLEM

As a devoted worker in the realm of church finance you know the difficulties of persuading some members to pay their fourth-quarter pledges.

8. POINT OUT HOW HE WILL GAIN AS AN INDIVIDUAL

The thing that makes it work so well in your behalf . . .

9. CHALLENGE HIM TO TRY SOMETHING

Discover all this and more when you attend the first meeting of the Camera Club Tuesday night.

10. ASK A QUESTION

Ever say to yourself, "I'm just spinning my wheels in life"?

11. START WITH GOOD NEWS

Yes, indeed, Mary, I'll be happy to write a letter of recommendation for you to Dean Roger Kelly at Duke University.

12. ACKNOWLEDGE HELP, SUGGESTION, COURTESY

Thank you for your thoughtful letter of July 2.

13. USE A CONVERSATIONAL PHRASE TO EMPHASIZE A POINT
    Make no mistake . . .

14. ACKNOWLEDGE A GIFT
    We are very grateful for your offering of $10. We shall convert it at once into our program of chairs, tables, maps, brightly painted walls, and all the comforts and necessities so vital to the success of our junior high department. And, of course, that is just why you have given it. You have only to walk through this place in about three weeks to see the good your kindness has accomplished and the happiness it has brought.

15. CONGRATULATE ON PERSONAL ACHIEVEMENT
    CONGRATULATIONS! All of us are so grateful to you for directing the projects of our senior high group in winning the leadership banner at the state rally in Louisville last week.

16. USE INCIDENT OR ANECDOTE
    This has probably happened to you: A few nights ago a man in Seattle was surprised when the telephone rang about midnight.

17. ACCENT LOVE AND DEVOTION TO OTHERS
    To you she's the loveliest girl who ever said, "I do." You want to give her the world, the moon, and the stars. And you would like her to have them forever—no matter what may happen to you.

18. SHOW A PLEASANT FUTURE
    You'll enjoy working with Roy Emerson because he is everything a Sunday school superintendent should be: dedicated, enthusiastic, helpful, creative

and with so much Christian joy that he inspires all who know him.

How can you acquire "you-ability"? As a minister you must have a deep feeling for others because your supreme interest centers in human beings. As Raymond Calkins says in *The Eloquence of Christian Experience*, "He [the minister] may possess all other qualifications . . . but above all, beyond all and within all, he must have an absorbing interest in the lives and souls of men."

Obviously, if you know the reader personally, then it is easier to form a mental image. In some situations you must visualize a person who is probably typical of the group.

Call it what you will—research, fact-finding, planning, digging—but spend plenty of time on the reader's side of the fence. That's where he lives and thinks. That's where you must reach him.

Look at this paragraph from a recent church letter:

> We are pleased to announce that we are now able to provide a larger parking lot for all of our members. We recognized the growing demand for this facility so that we could do more for our members. Our new lot is located near the Tenth Street entrance so that it will be convenient for all of our members.

Granted, the pastor was proud of the new lot. That's human. But he should have emphasized the value of the reader. He forgot to spotlight "the other fellow."

You're enthusiastic about your task of and the worth of religious values. That's natural. But whatever you are stressing, you must see the idea from the reader's point of view. You must tune in on people. Halford E. Luccock in his book *In the Minister's Workshop* emphasized this by saying, "Unless the sense of great issues is coupled with an equally vivid sense of people and their predicaments, with a knowledge of and sympathy for the bewildering range and variety of the needs, anxieties, and disturbances of individuals, the preacher's range will be sadly limited and his ministry circumscribed."

Can you really know how the reader will react to your letter before you mail it? Not exactly. But here's what a minister in North Carolina does: When time permits, he dictates a letter to be used in a mass mailing to all members. Then he mails it to himself at home! And then with fresh eyes and away from his study he makes some revisions. The result: a better letter. "You'd be surprised," he says, "how different a letter looks three or four days after it is written."

What's the first step in finding your "you" approach? Study your reader. Find out what interests him—what keeps him motivated. Then study your proposal to see how it can be made to tie into that interest. Use "you" as early in the letter as possible, and repeat it from time to time. You'll keep the reader involved. Result? You get reader identification and participation; you keep him in the spotlight.

4

SECRETS
of word magic

It's a funny thing, but most people grow cold and stiff when they start thinking about a letter. They hide their personality. They use pompous words—words they would never think of using in conversation.

Your letter may be written on your church letterhead which is beautiful and distinctive. It may answer all of the questions your reader wants to know. It may be spaced exactly right and meet all mechanical requirements. But if it lacks the magic ingredient of your personality—if it lacks the human touch—it is dead.

You are beginning to see now that, more than anything else, letter writing is a business of words, willing words that give your letters a tone and a pull that makes them powerful. As a minister you become an effective letter writer through the mastery of words, words which enable you to transmit thought, feelings, concepts, and emotions to the reader.

Note how words rise up and shine in this message released by the Advertising Council in its Religion in America campaign entitled "How to Build a Boy":

Mix several old tin cans full of fun, with a wild mop of hair. Blend in scuffed knuckles and knees, a missing tooth (optional). Then sprinkle in streaks of orneriness, pride, courage, envy, and maybe even a little fear (everybody knows that empty house down the block is haunted.)
And there: you've made a boy.

Well, almost.

Boys, wonderfully, have a sweet sense of the bigness and beauty and mystery of things. It's this sense of bigness and mystery we hope they'll never lose.

Religion is an awfully big word to a little boy. But the spirit of it isn't. And it's the spirit of religion that can bring peace, comfort, security and goodness to a boy—his whole life through.

Your children should worship this week in your church or synagogue. And the best way to see to it is to be there with them yourself.[1]

Read that again and you'll see how the writer used specific word pictures (a missing tooth, scuffed knuckles and knees, the empty house, a wild mop of hair). It's concreteness; it's getting down to people, cases, facts, colors, sensations, sounds, scenes, movement, dialogue, and events. Your letter carries more impact when you focus on the visible, the audible, and the measurable.

Good writing involves more than commas and periods, what words to use, and how to make an outline. Rather it is a deep feeling for reality—a feeling for people and things, for baseball, lodge meetings, TV detectives, county fairs, women's hats, apple pie, band music, and variety stores.

Your letters will carry word magic if you make every word and every phrase easy for the reader to understand. Rely on simple words. For example, you may write, "Too many cooks spoil the broth." But if you want to make it tough you can write, "Undue multiplicity of personnel assigned either concurrently or consecutively to a single function involves deterioration of quality in the resultant product as compared with the product of the labor of an exact sufficiency of personnel."

In school we were forced to learn rules about writing—ways

[1] Used by permission.

of punctuating, spelling, usage, and other standards. Yard-
sticks of grammar are important. But those aren't enough;
we must strive for a psychological approach. We must aim at
the heart. Letters are written to interpret, explain, persuade,
inform. If they don't accomplish their purpose, their literary
value is of little consequence. So we must concentrate on
words—right words—honest words. Furthermore, each word
must say exactly what you want it to say at the right time.
Words are your answers in the battle for attention; you must
learn to use them.

When you hear a letter writer say, "Now, if I just had the
words to express this idea," it's ten to one that he is hunting
for words when he really needs ideas. Perhaps he doesn't understand the facts, but it's more likely he doesn't have enough
of them.

Nor is that all. Before the words start flowing from his typewriter, he must have enough facts; he must understand them;
and he must organize them mentally or on paper so they will
come in the proper sequence. Then his imagination begins
to work and ideas germinate from the facts.

Can you "feel" a situation? If you can, your letter will have
a heart. Great writers remind us that meditation always pre-
cedes inspiration. You must absorb your material—facts, ideas,
possible tone—before the first word of the letter is typed.

As a minister you must be extremely careful to avoid an
"elegance" in writing and speaking. Many years ago Henry
Ward Beecher emphasized this by saying, "Above all other
men, the preacher should avoid what may be called a literary
style, as distinguished from a natural one; and by a 'literary
style,' technically so called, I understand one in which abound
these two elements—the artificial structure of sentences, and
the use of words and phrases peculiar to literature alone, and
not to common life."

29

KEEP MARCHING WITH IDEAS

Before you can make your letter move, you must know exactly where you are going. You must ask yourself, "What is the specific purpose of this letter?" In other words, you must know where you are going, why you are headed in that direction, and how you will get there.

Good organization makes ideas move, flow. And with a plan your words will carry the reader from your opener through a logical development to the desired conclusion. But your letter won't move if you use awkward sentences, vague words and phrases, weak logic, unbelievable statements, and improper transition.

Just as you plan the organization of a sermon, you do not write a letter until first of all you have determined your objective and then decided which is the most logical, effective, and desirable way to achieve that objective.

And after you've started to write, don't jump back and forth over the same idea. Say it and go forward. Get to the next idea and the next, always on a bee-line toward your goal, creating a well-constructed message which gets the reaction, the assent, and the agreement you want from your reader.

You must work for easy reading. You must avoid everything that can either slow up the reading or send your reader off on some side line of thought. Arm your words with power and your letter will ring true.

MAKE EVERY WORD CARRY ITS PART OF THE LOAD

Often at letter-writing clinics I have asked students to boil down the essentials of a letter to fifty words or less. And some exclaim, "Why, that's impossible. That's too much ground to cover." Then I invite them to study the story of the creation. Simple, moving, incredibly beautiful, the whole story is told in forty-six words: "In the beginning God created the heaven and the earth. And the earth was without form, and void; and darkness was upon the face of the deep. And the spirit of God moved upon the face of the waters. And God said, Let there be light" (Gen. 1:1-3).

Let's remember that words are time to the reader. Too many of them discourage his attention and kill his interest. And too many of them also bury important ideas under a verbal avalanche and sacrifice clearness to confusion. William H. Butterfield, authority on letter writing, reminds us that "any word that makes no contribution to the meaning of a sentence is a verbal parasite. Don't let verbal termites weaken the structure of your letters." Make every word count!

WORK TO FIND THE RIGHT WORDS

Your letter is more than so many words strung together. It must be correct in sentence structure and free from slipshod phrases. If it does have faulty construction, your reader's attention swings away from what he is reading and comes to focus on the offending error.

Can you really say what you mean? If you can't, you may turn out sentences like the following:

The Reverend J. T. Darrow spoke briefly much to the delight of the congregation.

I am glad to tell you that Gomer Hanks worked for me for seven years as a custodian, and I honestly believe him to be capable of anything.

Our church library offers you the opportunity of enjoying inspirational, worthwhile books every night but Monday.

Not one of these sentences expresses what the writer intended to say. In each case haste and carelessness produced a meaning that made the writer appear ridiculous. Just a little

31

care would have prevented these mirth-provoking statements. Be sure that every letter carrying your signature is correct.

STUDY AND ANALYZE GREAT WRITING

With all of the demands upon you you must take time for reading. Unless you rub elbows with great writers of all ages, you will never learn the magic of words. As you study your Bible, remember that nothing in all literature equals its clarity, power, and drama. Pull an old O. Henry book from your shelves, and see how he makes a fascinating story from a trivial incident. Study Charles Dickens and see how he makes characters come alive. Analyze today's best seller. Watch words at work in advertisements. To sum up: Respond to good writing whenever you find it. Then you'll see how words work for the masters.

And now let's look at some outstanding examples. Philip Wylie: "Lightning struck a graph in the sky." Time: "A grin like a Texas river, a mile wide and an inch deep." John Steinbeck: "The cat sitting in a circle of his tail." Jean B. Mosley: "Green meadows pinned down with dandelion brooches." Bess Streeter Aldrich: "Time, the careless laundryman, shrinks many of our ideals."

As you see, a great writer must have ideas, experiences, or thoughts. Then he possesses a mastery of words so that he can transmit exactly what he wants to transmit. Not words as words, but the concepts, the feelings, the sentiments, and the sensations for which the words stand.

In the finals, remember that words—willing words—carry your message. In weighing their content, we must know their intent. And words should be weighed, not counted. Don't try to write a letter; just try to say something. And when you say it with conviction your reader will respond because of the magic in your words.

5

HOW TO
click with your close

Your final sentence in your letter is read last—and remembered longest.

When a letter has arrested a reader's attention, captured his interest, awakened his desire to respond to your idea, and made him believe in your proposal, there is still a job to be done. That's getting the reader to act, to do something.

Next to the opening of the letter the ending is the position of most emphasis. It's easy to end a letter, of course, but it is quite difficult to write a close which induces action, which swings the reader around to your way of thinking. To be smoothly rounded out, the last lines of a letter must bring the reader over to your side.

Your closing can accomplish many things. It can, for instance, bring your message into clear focus: "May we ask you to return this report by October 16?" It gives you a chance to say something genuinely pleasant: "It was a thrill to talk to you on the phone this morning" or "I'm glad to have been able to help." It can offer more than your reader asked of you: "If you'd like more information about this, let me know. I'll be glad to see that you get it." Or it can say, quite simply: "Every best wish."

Try this: Before you start your next letter ask yourself, "What is this letter intended to accomplish? What do I want it to do?" Keep the answer in mind, and you are more likely to end up with an effective closing.

Another method is to write the ending first. You write the

33

action-demanding paragraph first. Then go back and build toward the closing so that the letter reaches a climax at the end. Try this and see how it gives your letter cohesion, movement, and purpose.

To be sure, not all letters make the same use of the climax. In many church situations your letter is not an attempt to "sell" anything but is merely a warm, friendly note. But even then a mechanical, stereotyped ending leaves a flat impression. Whatever type of letter you plan, see that the ending brings the recipient to the proper pitch of enthusiasm, and then he will make the desired response.

For a moment let's visualize the reader as he comes to the end of your letter. You aren't standing near to answer his questions and excuses. Mere words on paper are carrying the entire load of your proposal. The reader must say "yes" or "no." You can't say, "Before you decide, there's one fact I failed to mention." You have made your speech to the jury, there's no appealing the case. What will the verdict be?

Most writers fizzle out at the end of the letter. Too many of them are uncertain about how or when to stop. Somehow they can't make this pivot point strong enough to win good will, solve a situation, interpret a problem, or inspire positive feelings.

Read a stack of letters, and you'll see that many writers use a perfunctory close rather than making the final impression count. For example, glance at the following endings:

Hoping that you'll consider the matter and that you'll attend the reception for Mrs. Gatchel, I am,

Sincerely yours,

Assuring you that your cooperation will be greatly appreciated, I am,

Yours very truly,

Trusting this information is to your satisfaction, I am,
Sincerely yours,

Rather than keeping up the momentum of the letter so that the finish will be strong and clear-cut, each of those just fades out with a complimentary close. Revised to modern practice the foregoing examples might read as follows:

We'll be looking for you at the reception!

Your help will be greatly appreciated.

Hope you find this information useful in writing your feature story on early churches of Middletown. Can we be of further help?

BEWARE OF USING THE PARTICIPIAL CLOSE

Nothing destroys the effectiveness of a letter quite so much as a participial close. Instead of terminating the message in a forceful yet friendly manner it slows the letter down and actually decreases the power which has gone before.

Avoid endings like the following:

Trusting this meets with your satisfaction,

Hoping to see you in church next Sunday, I am,

Thanking you in advance for accepting this position,

In many letters you try to get the reader to take action while the effect of the letter is strong. For the longer he delays, the weaker the impulse will become. At times he may lose your letter, intending to act later. On another occasion he may feel that he should respond at once, but he postpones the action. You must hurry his "good intentions" into action.

You must often give your reader a jog so that he will take the desired action. And it will take all of the ingenuity at your command to give him reasons why it will pay him to take action at once. Show him what he will gain, or what he will lose in waiting. Perhaps this will be his only opportunity. Show how much he is needed. Stress the "you" benefits—benefits which will help him—in the close.

To make your conclusion effective, be certain that the whole thought of your letter is crystallized in definite and clear-cut words. If you are requesting some action, the close of the paragraph should state briefly, very specifically, and yet courteously, just what you want the reader to do.

"Extra urges" usually speed the response when a prompt reply is needed. By setting a deadline, the last sentence may nudge a reader into action. So if you can give a good reason for a prompt reply, it will help.

Note: A prompt reply will be appreciated.

But: I must have reports from all officers for the annual report which goes to the printer June 3. I'll be grateful if you'll rush me your summary of activities before then.

AVOID TRITE ENDINGS

It's easy to write a "formula close." Perhaps the phrase was good years ago, but it has been used so much that it is practically meaningless. And if used, it makes your letter sag at the very point it should get a lift. Look how you can strengthen worn-out endings:

Weak: We wish to thank you for your interest in our Youth Fellowship and to assure you that we stand ready to help you at all times.

Better: If you have a special problem, Mrs. Lee Chandler, director of religious education, will be glad to help you. Feel free to call her or visit her at any time.

Weak: We hope this arrangement will be satisfactory.

Better: This arrangement will give you time to choose

staff members to assist you in the Vacation Bible School.

Weak: We hope you will receive this special music soon.

Better: You should receive this shipment of music by February 15—in plenty of time to start rehearsals for the Easter cantata.

AVOID TOO MANY CHOICES

Unless you are careful, you may sometimes confuse the reader by offering him a choice of actions. And if you confuse him, you are likely to delay his decision—if he makes one. Note the following:

If you will sign the enclosed card indicating when you wish to attend one of the stewardship dinners, Miss Brenda Dodd, our church secretary, will confirm your reservation; or if you had rather, you may call her at JA 4-6754 and tell her. Should you happen to drop by the church during the next few days, drop by her office (just down the hall east from the associate pastor's office) and tell her of your decision. Or watch for a reservation coupon in the *Tower Chimes*, our church paper, May 7 or 14.

Apparently the writer had not planned his letter, so the ending is a mixture of suggestions. How would you have responded—if at all? One definite urge and not more than two would have made an effective ending.

SELECT FROM THREE ACTION CLOSINGS

In letters seeking action you may use one of three types of close—command, suggestion, or question. The command type, of course, gives the strongest urge, because it is the most direct.

37

Many letter writers feel, however, that through overuse it has lost some of its appeal, so they rely chiefly on a less insistent invitation to act. Here are examples of the three types:

1. COMMAND:

Call Mr. Riker today (PE 4-7554) and tell him that you'll attend.

Be sure to sign the reservation card and mail it today!

2. SUGGESTION:

Try to be there, and bring along any suggestions or ideas that you might want to present.

I am looking forward to hearing from you in the near future.

The enclosed card is a convenient way to say, "Show me."

3. QUESTION:

Won't you let us hear from you at once?

Can we serve you further?

Can you let me know by March 15 whether you can serve as chairman of this important committee?

SPEED UP RESPONSE

In special campaigns you may use coupons, cards, ready-stamped envelopes, and other reply forms with letters. A card may be enclosed with the letter, or it may be affixed at the bottom of the letterhead. When this is done, never allow the card to cover any of the letter itself. A stamped envelope is effective in bringing back a reply, because it suggests the importance of an answer and the fact that one is expected. In every instance gear the copy on the reply form to that of your letter.

Why this emphasis on reply forms? Just this: In a special situation the last paragraph of your letter must do more than ask for action. It must spell out exactly what the reader should do to take such action. For example, if a reply card is enclosed you might say:

Remember, God blesses those who place him first. So sign your pledge card and use the enclosed postage-paid envelope to return it to the church. Drop it in the mail today.

It pays to give all of those details, because test after test has shown that if you fail to tell the reader about the card, what to put on the card, and what to do with the card, results will drop. Why? "It isn't because people are stupid," Ferd Nauheim, letter-writing authority, explains. "It's because the impulse to take the requested action hangs by a slender, delicate thread. You cannot afford to add one bit of weight to the request hanging on the end of that thread."

Whether you are using a separate card or a coupon to be torn from a letter or folder, you can use a variety of action urges. Speed up your responses by using some of these in your card and coupon copy:

1. UTILIZE THE FIRST PERSON
   I want to know more about the World Mission program.
   I want to step up my effectiveness as a teacher so please send me, *Secrets of Successful Teaching.*

2. DESCRIBE THE PHYSICAL ACTION
   Just mail coupon.
   Tear along the dotted line.
   Place in the mail today.

3. UTILIZE FREE-BOOKLET TECHNIQUE
   Rush illustrated brochure, *The Cross in My Pocket.*

Please send me literature describing the summer church camps.

4. EMPHASIZE EASE OF REPLY

Postage-free reply form is enclosed.

This coupon is for your convenience.

Just sign the card and drop it in the mail today.

5. INSPIRE CONFIDENCE

Once you experience the blessings which come from this activity, I believe you, too, will attend every Prayer Breakfast.

6. ASSUME AGREEMENT

Yes! Count on me to help in the visitation campaign.

Yes, indeed, our Senior House does need new furniture so I'll be happy to . . .

7. HASTEN THE ACTION

Don't delay—mail today.

To be sure of a reservation, send the card at once!

Deadline for tickets Tuesday, April 10!

8. ASK A QUESTION

Why not start your subscription with the January issue?

You'll find this experience most rewarding. Won't you put me to the test?

MAKE MORE USE OF "SPIRIT-LIFTERS"

Sometimes no action is sought in your ending. Rather, you stress something pleasant—something positive. You use what one minister termed "spirit-lifters." Here are examples from pastors' letters:

All good wishes to you in your new position.

We're always glad to be of service.

We truly appreciate your cooperation in this great privilege which is ours in the building of Christ's kingdom through our church.

Let us pray that the Lord will lead us in our missionary efforts this year.

Thank you for your loyalty and your devotion.

May God's richest blessings abide upon you always, and in all ways, I pray.

The Lord bless you and keep you.

God bless you richly.

The Lord bless you and may your life ever be a blessing to the church, I pray.

May God's richest blessings be upon you as you take your places in the full stream of our church life. And may your lives ever be a blessing to his name.

Yours in the April-spirit of risen lives!

Best wishes for a wonderful New Year!

God bless you all.

The Christian church needs your support at this time in history. We must show the world where we stand.

With every good wish and may God bless you in your work.

God give you and yours the joys of the coming holiday season.

May the love of the Lord be very real to you.

May God continue to bless you richly for assuming as your responsibility a part in this program. We move forward in faith and gratitude.

41

May God bless you and guide you in this important decision.

Blessings on you for a wonderful Christmas season.

Congratulations and all good wishes for many happy tomorrows.

Remember these four ideas when ending your letter:

1. Make every word in your close count. Make it direct, friendly.
2. Remember, your closing should signify something—something pertinent to the message, to the needs of the reader—in other words, something meaningful and appropriate.
3. Avoid the use of clichés—worn "dead ends."
4. Know when to stop—and how.

Put these into practice and your ending will be the verbal equivalent of a friendly handshake and a smiling good-bye written in the belief that "all's well that ends well."

6

HOW TO
pretest your letters

Imagine for a moment that you're peeking over the shoulder of Mr. Church Member as he reads your letter. He scans part of it. Then he reads the rest. Then he tosses it away. Why?

Maybe you forgot to make an outline before you dictated the letter. Perhaps you just put so many words together and the result was dull and flat. Working in a rush, you forgot to isolate one basic idea. And it's possible that you assembled the facts in terms of reader interest and not your own. By now you are probably asking, "Can you really pretest letters?"

First, it must be admitted that whether a letter hits the target or misses depends on countless things. Some of these factors are easily seen—others are intangible. Maybe your reader has a headache. Perhaps he receives so much mail that he has a negative feeling toward all letters. Maybe he is so busy that he doesn't have time to concentrate on your message. There is no way in which his reaction can be predicted. But sound planning will boost the impact of your letters.

To be successful as a minister you must possess a thorough knowledge of mankind in general and of your own congregation in particular. Many years ago Phillips Brooks advised ministers to "know your congregation as thoroughly as you can." Batsell Barrett Baxter in his book *The Heart of the Yale Lectures* says "that to know men deeply the minister must live among them, observing every phase of human behavior.

Only by living close to men can he learn the innermost workings of their minds, and only then does he know how to take aim with the message of God." This deep concern for your congregation is a tremendous help in letter writing.

But that isn't enough. Reader response cannot always be predicted because so many factors are involved in letter writing—physical appearance, tone, timing, approach, reader interest, nature of the message, and numerous others. But we can use some tested pointers and thus avoid many pitfalls in church correspondence. By using these basic principles you can raise the effectiveness of your letters. Planning always pays.

If you want your letter to click, you must plan it step by step. Many of the situations handled in pastoral letters are so similar that one approach serves for all. But even a little touch —some phrase or sentence which gives the reader an emotional lift—in a so-called routine letter makes that extra planning most effective.

In a complicated-letter situation planning is vital. "I learned a long time ago," a pastor, well-known for his successful letters, said, "that a letter tossed off in five minutes may be the very one which results in misunderstanding and more problems. Now I often take thirty minutes or more to plan, dictate, and then revise one which makes the recipient feel better towards me and the church." So time required in planning is often determined by the uniqueness of the problem and how soon an effective solution can be found.

With the tempo of life so speeded up, you may get into the habit of dictating scores of poorly planned messages. Even when you feel rushed, take time to consider these steps:
1. Objective: What kind of response am I seeking?
2. Function: What fact-finding, deliberation, research must be done to assure that response?
3. Appeal: What appeal or combination of appeals shall I use?

4. Keynote: What will be the theme and aim of my message?
5. Point of contact: How shall I tie up the message to the interests of the reader?
6. Tone: What "tone of voice" shall I use to get the desired response?

Even when you follow these steps, remember that the success of your letter will depend for the most part on your creative ingenuity. But by following even a simple plan you can get your ideas better organized, consider the relationship of each to the others, and see your letter as a whole.

MAKE EVERY WORD COUNT

Are you a word waster? Probably. That's normal because letter experts tell us that about 30 percent of the words in a typical letter are excess baggage.

What happens when you use too many words? For one thing your reader may resent any letter which requires him to wade through a mass of unnecessary verbiage because you were too careless and hurried to present your ideas concisely.

Before you know it you may get into the habit of using too many words. Paul Scherer in his book, *For We Have This Treasure*, pleads for ministers to organize sermon material and then says, "Having nothing to say which has seemed to you of sufficient importance to compel a clear analysis, you fill in the necessary time with a few remarks. You aim at nothing in particular, and hit it squarely in the middle."

Here are a few excerpts that lack terminal facilities. Each example is followed by a revision that expresses the same idea more quickly and forcefully in fewer words:

If you can think of any other way in which we can be of service to you at any time, please get in touch with us because we'll be happy to come to your aid. (35 words)

45

Please call on us whenever we can be of service. (10 words)

It is my purpose at this time to send you my congratulations upon the excellent and unusual way in which you planned and supervised the annual Christmas party for our Sunday school teachers. (33 words)

Congratulations on the fine way you directed our Christmas party! (10 words)

I wish to take this occasion to express our appreciation. (10 words)

Thank you! (2 words)

Note the many superflous words in the original versions, and then see how the revised sentences, shorter and to the point, are much more forceful.

A word of caution: You may strive so hard to be brief that you may destroy good will instead of building it. It's like this: Without thinking, you may give your reader a "brush-off." Beware of any emphasis on briefness alone; because it should never be used at the expense of clearness, courtesy, and completeness.

WRITE TO JOHN JONES

Your letter will get results only as you talk to a person on paper. This principle works in every letter situation, whether you are writing a single message or a letter to be used in a mass mailing to your congregation.

"Our sense of personal importance resents a letter that ranks us as one or two billion other people," Don Ross emphasized in an article in *Advertising & Selling*. And then he continues, "How much more complimentary is the mailing piece that says, 'You, Mr. John Jones, are the only person in the world I'm interested in right now.'"

What's the first hurdle toward reader interest? Let's repeat it: Know your reader. Ask yourself, "What's his goal in life? How does he differ from other persons? What is his interest in the church? How can I catch and hold his attention? How can the church serve him?" You can't just guess what he is like. You must know him.

Once you have isolated some of the motives and appeals, select one or more of the stronger ones. One type of letter may concentrate on one of them—a single strong motive. For example, you may use a letter to show the joy of tithing. In another, several motives may be combined with one predominant theme with other motives as secondary. Once you find some predominant motives, then your letter can show how these desires can be realized.

You may recall the classic story about Gladstone, once Prime Minister of England. "Why," chided the great man, "don't you listen when I speak to you?" "Because," replied the youthful Queen Victoria, "you talk to me as if I were a public meeting."

Don't make the same mistake. In every letter talk to one person—write to John Jones.

MAKE YOUR LETTER BELIEVABLE

Grandma Cochran has never taken a course in correspondence. Nor has she ever read a book on letter writing. But how her personality shines through her letters! This is vital because there's no substitute for the human touch—the touch that gives a letter personality, friendliness, and believability.

To make a letter believable (like a sermon) you must write from the heart. Your letters gain a new persuasive power when you speak with sincerity. This quality was emphasized by Edwin DuBose Mouzon in his book, *Preaching with Authority,* when he said, "First, there must be sincerity. The

47

preacher is a communicator. His convictions pass in some strange way over into the minds of his hearers. . . . If he is a man of strong faith, his faith will flow down into others."

This isn't a matter, you see, of trick phrases, clever words, and gimmicks. Rather you get this feeling—this feeling of sincerity—into your letters only as you experience in it. James Edward Freeman in his book, *The Ambassador*, emphasizes this quality by stating that "the message of value must be the expression of our own deep and unfailing conviction. It cannot be the expression of what someone else has felt or experienced; it must be our own."

SPEAK THE READER'S LANGUAGE

Your message must depend on words—willing words. Some of them are dull and slow. Some are crisp, harsh, sharp. And some words are warmhearted and friendly. Words are the key to everything in man's civilization. Their vital function is stressed by John D. Yeck and John T. Maguire in their book, *Planning and Creating Better Direct Mail:* "A man lives by words. A man loves by words. A man prays with words. And a man dies for, by, and with words."

You hold your reader's attention in two ways: first, by what you say; and second, by how you say it. This means that your preliminary planning must include vocabulary research. Not only should the entire letter be written in the respondent's language, but you should also seek to use the particular words or expressions which he uses when speaking of the particular subject of your letter.

Without thinking, you may use words and phrases of your calling, much to the bewilderment of the reader who is unversed in such terminology. Steer clear of expressions like "apostolic succession," "messianic," "Magnificat," "canonicity," "eschatology" and "pseudepigraphal books." Your reader doesn't have time to consult a Bible commentary every time he receives one of your letters.

GEAR YOUR MESSAGE TO THE SITUATION

When you are planning a letter, forget the temptation to do it quickly. Instead, study your proposal, the reader, and the unique circumstances of the particular situation. Take a long look at some of the basic motivations of the reader and the appeals which might be used in tapping those motivations. Armed with these facts, you can visualize the framework of your letter.

As you plan your letter, select simple words; for these move the hearts of men. Slang? Occasionally it may express an idea vividly and exactly. But some readers might consider it undignified. Humor, when used with care, can sometimes add to a letter's effectiveness. In whatever tone you are writing, select words which convey vivid sense imagery. You can do this by using words which force the reader to seem to feel, to experience the thing you are talking about. It's like this:

Weak: Come to church next Sunday!

Better: You'll get a new lift for your life when you come next Sunday!

Your reader will always react in the desired way as long as you give him the feeling: "This is important to me . . . this is worthwhile." As long as you give him the feeling that he "is there"—involved and participating in what you are suggesting—and talk to him in his language, you can keep up strong identification.

ALWAYS BE TACTFUL

Whether the purpose of your letter is to grant a request, step up stewardship, or ask for help, there is no substitute for

49

tact if the job is to be done effectively. Here's a simple test: Right after you have written the letter, step into the reader's shoes. Does the message contain any words, phrases, or sentences that would irritate you? If it does, then smooth off those rough spots before mailing it.

Let's look at the tactless statement and then see how it might be revised:

Original: You are making a serious mistake in soliciting books for the church library during this vacation period.

Revision: Since so many of our folk are out of the city in August, they would probably respond much quicker to your fine project later this fall.

Don't you agree that the revision presents the same thought just as clearly without conveying the disagreeable implication of the first statement? As you see, the revision shows a courteous consideration of the reader and a little more care in phraseology. But hurried letter writers often overlook this consideration and care, with a consequent loss of good will.

GIVE YOUR LETTER "EYE APPEAL"

What kind of first impression will your letter make? What does it look like? These are important questions because the reader gets a psychological impression the moment he sees your letter. Paper, design, and color have an impact on the eye and sense of touch. Choice of type, weight and quality of the paper, and the quality of reproduction which produces the reading matter at the top of the page—all these should give an impact, a stature, a prestige to you and your church.

Your letterhead's design should be developed upon the basis of these principles: It should limit the content to essential information, should be simple in design, and should have an element of individuality (your printer, engraver, or some other competent person can help you). A drawing of your church is usually preferable to a halftone cut made from a photograph.

You must, of course, choose an envelope which harmonizes with your letterhead. This means that the typography, weight and quality of paper, color and other factors of the envelope must be in keeping with your letterhead. Just be sure that the envelope design is in keeping with the mission of the church and that it is an expression of that quest.

Summing up this important chapter—important enough to be read several times—let's boil it down to these highlights:

1. When the planning is right, the purpose is right.
2. Use a planned approach, not a canned approach.
3. Only the right words possess the power to stir men's minds.
4. You'll jump the highest hurdle in letter writing when you stop talking to yourself and start talking to Mr. Reader.
5. The best letter is always written from an educated heart.

7

EXTRAS
to give letters a lift

Readership surveys keep reminding us of this fact: You must give the reader something of value in exchange for the time it takes to read your letter. Sometimes you can promise benefits, satisfactions, rewards. At other times you can convince the reader—through empathy—that you understand his situation. On other occasions you can keep the reader going your way by using words that rise up and shine.

You can name other ways of stepping up readership. But sooner or later you face this question: How can I reduce the number of dull, innocuous, colorless, insensate letters?

Let's remind ourselves of this fact: A letter which is interesting and exciting is one which relates directly to a problem or interest of the reader and is written in language that evokes an emotional response.

If you've wondered what is the most important trait of all topflight letter writers, it's this: a good associative faculty. This is your ability to see relationships. It's the knack of bridging the gap between you and your reader.

"Writing an effective letter isn't a matter of literary mechanics," a minister, well-known for his writing, declares. "Rather, it's a matter of feeling—of caring for people . . . ordinary people."

And this is almost as vital: If you seek creative freshness, you cannot operate with a limited number of devices and approaches. In your deep concern for others you will step up your knowledge of psychology, because as you live with them you learn what makes them tick. This feeling for people—this understanding of human motivation—usually separates the mediocre letter writer from the master.

How can you get letters out of the rut on the high road to readership? Here are some ways of giving them a lift:

1. TRY THE UNCONVENTIONAL FOR A CHANGE OF PACE

Not too many moons ago experts said, "The ideal letter never runs more than a page." Then someone reversed the trend and, plagiarizing Abraham Lincoln, compared the length of a letter to the length of a man's legs: "They should be long enough to reach the ground," meaning they can be as long as they must be to reach the point. Soon afterwards longer and longer letters were written, and they produced results. So instead of falling into the "everybody's doing it" theme, break tradition. Refuse to fall into a lockstep. Break tradition. Do not be different just to be daring. Dare to be different to be distinctive.

2. TRY A SENSORY AID

Here's what one minister did: He put an attractive bookmark in his letter urging daily Bible readings. You can dramatize the showing of a special film by stapling a small piece of film in one of the upper corners of your letter. So do this: Be on the lookout for nonverbal forms of communication—color, shape, illustration, devices—which provoke sensory reactions.

3. PEP UP THE LOOKS OF YOUR LETTERS

It's amazing what a few dots, some underlined words, capital letters and dashes will do in stepping up the appearance of your letter. Oh, sure, there's always danger of going to the extreme. But let's remember that capitalization, dashes, indented paragraphs, underlined words and phrases, l e t t e r s p a c i n g (just like that)—these are to letters what inflection is to the voice. How boring it is to listen to someone who talks in a monotone! Even if he speaks with the wisdom of Solomon, you miss the force and meaning of his statements unless you pay close attention. Letters can be monotones, too, so put L I F E into them—inflection, if you please—by means of "type-ical" emphasis.

4. USE THE PERSON'S NAME FROM TIME TO TIME

Seldom, if ever, Mrs. Higgins, have I heard such a stirring performance of *The Messiah* as the one which you directed Sunday night.

Keep up your excellent efforts, Jim, because with you spearheading the drive we are about to reach a new high in membership in the Men's Breakfast Club.

I sincerely hope, Mrs. Gebbie, that you'll enjoy the challenges and satisfactions which will be yours in serving as chairman of the literature committee.

Most of all, Gerald, if there is anything I can do to help, just say the word!

5. TRY A HOMELY EXPRESSION OR TWO

You've already told yourself as you plan your letter, "Now I'm going to talk to this person." In doing this you'll skip any temptation to use stilted words or theological phrases. But you won't keep your personaltiy under cover. Instead, say what you want to say by using a few homely words and expressions which fit the tone of your message. You know these expressions—these man-to-man expressions—because you probably use some of them in conversation.

Phrases like, "You can bet your bottom dollar," "Sure hope our paths cross again," "Keep up the good work!" "Stay right in there and pitch," and "Hope this year is the best ever."

When do you use one of these? (a) If it's pertinent, and (b) if it makes an interesting friendly letter.

6. SOUND A CHEERFUL NOTE

Letters are like people; the cheerful, enthusiastic ones win more friends than the neutral type. So it's only human nature to like a letter writer whose enthusiasm, hope, and cheer show through. Henry Ward Beecher reminded us years ago that "the approach which we make to men's consciences and feelings in religion must be made in such a way as to excite in them, not combativeness, not resistance, but hope and aspiration." Proclaim the good news of the gospel in your letters.

7. TRY A "P.S." FOR ADDED PUNCH

Chances are you've asked yourself, "Shall I ever use a postscript intentionally?" If so, when? One way: Use a handwritten postscript in certain types of letters. It can give your letter a personal flavor and zest (even in a sizeable mass mailing). Keep it short. Make it personal. Here are a few examples:

P. S. Congratulations to John on receiving scholarship!

P. S. Let's get together for lunch during the convention.

P. S. Many mothers have told me how delighted they are that you have decided to remain as junior high superintendent.

P. S. You continue to amaze me with your many achievements.

P. S. With you at the helm, Arnold, our every-member canvas will be a tremendous success!

8. SHOWMANSHIP GETS ATTENTION

The chances are that most of your letters follow a fairly normal pattern, that is, that they look much like the rest of the mail your recipient gets. And this is as it should be. Occasionally you may run into a problem that needs a little more impact. You want your message to stand out—to be remembered. Before deciding to use any unusual letter ask yourself, "What effect will it have on the reader? Is the approach in keeping with the objective?" Now for an example: A Maryland pastor, needing money to repaper the walls of the nursery, sent brief typed notes to twenty persons on sections of the old, faded paper. Result! Enough money to repaper the room and repaint the woodwork. Then there was the Arizona pastor who used sheets of graph paper for letterheads to remind finance committee members of the campaign's progress. "We wrapped up the whole thing in ten days," he reported. Be on the lookout for ways of using unusual letters. When carefully chosen they can bring results.

As you see from these ideas, you have great flexibility in the selection and use of attention-getting devices. Even in a mass mailing you can use letters to interpret your church with a "reader-only" individualism, with novelty, with realism.

8

MOVING
people to action

Your success as a minister rests largely on one thing: your ability to gain the cooperation of others.

"The real test of a minister's efficiency," Roy L. Smith wrote as editor of the *Christian Advocate*, "is not the amount of work he does, but the amount he is able to get his people to do. . . . To him the members of his congregation are the forces he has at his disposal—the capital he has to invest in the Kingdom."

As a minister you must spark the lives of your members to work and witness for Christ. "You shall be my witnesses." (Acts 1:8 RSV.) This is not a task to be confined to the pulpit or evangelists. "The phenomenal expansion of the early church," observes Robert J. McCracken, minister of Riverside Church, New York City, "was not the result solely of the preaching labors of men like Paul, Peter and John. On the side of human instrumentality it was due in the main to the inconspicuous and faithful witness of a multitude of anonymous folk."

You may advertise your services, multiply your organizations, start new activities, and increase the number of committees. But unless you use the early apostolic way of building up the church—friend talking to friend, relative talking with relative, neighbor with neighbor—then you miss the most effective way. Friendly letters can spur people to action.

Three things may happen when you get the cooperation and help of your members. First, each person who responds enjoys the recognition—the sense of performing a unique task —which comes from his assignment. Second, the greater the participation the greater the feeling of belonging and sharing in a great cause. Most important of all, many Christians find something that helps them live, and they want to pass it on. And when this happens the outreach of your church will touch the lives of many with pardon, peace, and power.

If you really want a working group, you know the necessity of contacting members personally, by using the telephone, or utilizing effective letters. In some instances, it is well to use all three methods. Whether combined with other sources or used alone, friendly letters do have a pulling power.

You'll get a better response with letters of request by doing two things: (a) Remember the reader's point of view, and (b) make every word lead the reader to the definite action which you desire.

As you see, your problem is to study your reader and find a point of contact with his interest and then show how your proposition can be made to tie into that interest. Think of the hurdles in his mind—any reasons he might decline—and then knock them over in your message.

Members are flattered when you ask their advice. Harry E. Hess, a Methodist minister for over fifty years, recalled in an article in *Christian Herald* what he would do differently if he started all over again. "I would ask more questions," he said. "The humblest person of my parish has something to contribute. . . . The parishioner likes to talk about himself. He feels honored if you ask him questions. Your reward is doubled, for you learn something from him and you win a friend."

The potential uses of the personal letter in getting action or advice (or both) are as numerous as the needs of the church. Avoid a hurried letter. Instead, seek to make each one forceful,

58

interesting, and convincing, and it will bring results. Here are examples of suitable letters:

Dear Mr. Wacker:

Maybe you noticed the quip of Frank Ward in his column, "Nearly News," the other night. He said, "The person who admits he has a lot to learn has already learned a lot."

We've tried to use that principle in the activities of Oak Cliff Presbyterian Church for years. We know we can always improve our program and thus strengthen the ministry of the church in this community.

As you know from your experience, there is quite a turnover of choir members. Some join, help for a few weeks, and then drop out. How can we motivate more folk to sing in the choir regularly? Is there anything that I or members of the church staff can do to keep choir membership at a regular level?

As a loyal member of the group for many years, you can help us with your suggestions. Send your suggestions to me; or better still, give me a call so that we can get together and share suggestions.

Your help will be greatly appreciated.

Sincerely yours,

Dear Mrs. Sommers:

A philosopher once wrote, "The wisdom we most admire is of those who come to us for advice."

But we're using that in reverse. We want your advice and wisdom. It's this way: St. John's will observe its seventy-fifth anniversary next year, and we want to make this observance eventful and inspirational.

We've written pastors of other churches that have held anniversary programs for their ideas. But we'd like for you

59

to suggest ways in which we might make this a truly memorable event.

Will you help us by indicating, on the back of this letter, any suggestions for making our anniversary a success? The prepaid envelope will bring your comments directly to me.

Your comments will be most helpful . . . and very much appreciated.

Cordially yours,

Dear Mr. Conger:

Ever say to yourself, "I wish I could edit one issue of 'The Lutheran Voice' "?

Well, whether you have ever considered the idea or not, we'd like so much to get your suggestions for improving the weekly publication.

Would you like more items about members? Various church groups? Short editorials? News about future plans of the church? More news of coming events? Stories on the status of the budget?

Your suggestions and comments will receive careful consideration because we are most anxious to make "The Lutheran Voice" of real interest to all members.

Jot down your ideas on the back of this sheet and place it in the enclosed reply envelope which requires no postage. I'll be looking for your suggestions.

Sincerely yours,

Dear Mr. Coston:

Will you favor us with a little advice?

We have been giving a lot of thought lately to ways in which we could step up the effectiveness of our youth program, particularly those activities planned for teen-agers.

Our church has a fine reputation for its youth program, but we feel that we could improve. And this is where we seek your advice.

We'd like to hear your comments and suggestions at a special meeting of teachers in the Wesley Room of the church at 7:30 Tuesday night.

Your comments will be most welcome.

Cordially yours,

Dear Edwin:

Did you see the recent cartoon of the little boy who asked his dad, "If it's really a small world, why does it cost so much to run it?"

Church members sometimes ask questions like that. Often they cannot see the outreach of the church in its worldwide ministry. They see the varied activities of the local church but find it hard to visualize the impact which is exerted through the hospitals, schools, missionaries, and other agencies.

How can we make our people more conscious of the global ministry of the church? We'll be anxious to hear your suggestions at a meeting of the missions board in the church library at 3 o'clock next Sunday afternoon, January 12.

We'll appreciate greatly your presence.

Sincerely yours,

Dear Fred:

Did you know that some of the electric circuits in our church are over forty years old? As a result, some are overloaded and the danger of fire is increasing, an electrical engineer told us after an inspection this week.

We should look into this immediately, so I'd like for you to attend a trustees meeting at the church next Monday night,

March 13, at 7:30. Jack Sterling, who made the inspection, will show us some of the danger spots.

Your help will be appreciated.

Cordially yours,

Dear Ronald:

Some writer recently observed, "Look at the irony of the situation; at a time when society has developed the best tools for communication no one has anything to say!"

Is this true of Christian communications? In a world of so much talk is the church speechless? Do we keep shouting the same message louder and louder? Does the church have something to say in these times?

You'll agree that these are vital questions—timely questions. Now: I'd like so much for you to serve as chairman of a committee on communications. With your expert know-how gained by working for years with various mediums, I know that you and fellow committee members can set up a more effective program for our church.

Yes, the church does have a great message to proclaim. And many are waiting to hear it. And I'm sure that your committee can suggest specific ways in which we can communicate the good news of the gospel.

Let's get together soon and choose other members of the committee. Your counsel and leadership will be deeply appreciated.

Sincerely yours,

Dear Glen:

During this year of emphasis on youth at St. Luke's every method and means available are being used to make possible the development of dedicated Christian young people. One approach has been to have a youth make a short talk at each Sunday evening service telling what Christ and the church mean in his or her life. This will continue.

Related to this, we are asking a few adults who hold important places in St. Luke's and in Oklahoma City to appear before the various youth groups on Sunday morning or evening to give an expression of their faith. You are one of these important persons. What you say can be of lasting benefit to youth.

Enclosed is information which may be helpful in preparing your talk. May we count on you in this very important undertaking?

Sincerely yours,[1]

Dear Malcolm:

Did you read this quip in a recent issue of a weekly magazine? "If we could see ourselves as others see us, we'd probably be surprised."

We'd like to be surprised. That's why we would welcome your suggestions for next year's programs for the Men's Brotherhood.

As you know, we have presented speakers, movies, musical programs, and demonstrations. Men of our church have responded by attending regularly, and we want to be sure that future programs will interest just as many men—and even more.

Can you think of any way in which we might improve our programming? If so, we'll be most grateful if you'll send us your suggestions. Your comments will help us in reaching more men in the year ahead. We'll look forward to hearing from you.

Sincerely yours,

[1] Used by W. McFerrin Stowe, while serving as pastor of St. Luke's Methodist Church, Oklahoma City, Okla.

Dear friends:

Christmas brings us so many joys that it is impossible to name all of them. We share many of the same thoughts during this season and yet each of us, in a sense, derives some unique feelings from Christmas.

This year, for the first time, my Christmas sermon will be prepared by members of the congregation. Not later than December 12, send me your comments on "What Christmas Means to Me." These comments will form the basis for my sermon for Sunday morning, December 23.

Your ideas will be welcomed.

Your minister,

Dear Harry:

Where is the First Presbyterian Church going?

This question struck me not long ago when I read in "Religion in Life" that Hans Hoffman made the statement that "the church is under the illusion that it is making progress, whereas in reality it is moving in a vicious circle."

Should we evaluate our total program? Should we take a long-term look at our future goals? Is our program meeting the needs of today's members? Are we going in a circle?

Since you have been so active in church life here, and especially in the overall activities, I would appreciate your investigation of these problems. I shall be glad to help you make plans and select members for a committee at any time convenient for you.

Cordially yours,

Dear Friend:

Time is running out—fast!

Yes, indeed, your subscription to "The Church Messenger" is running out. And it will soon unless we have your "okay" now!

64

Don't cut yourself off from getting . . .

tips on teaching from experts—new ways of finding fresh material for your lessons—how to use audio-visual aids effectively—tested ways of increasing attendance—PLUS many other informative and useful features.

. . . not when it takes just a minute to sign and return the enclosed postage-paid form back to me.

Send your renewal today! Don't let time run out completely. We'll bill you later if you wish. Or you can send the payment with the card. May we hear from you soon?

Sincerely yours,

Of all the elements in the action letter the basic reason to which the reader responds is the most important. As you have seen, this may be done in two ways. Sometimes you show the reader how he will benefit, what he will gain by responding. In other situations you may show what he will lose by not responding. If you aren't careful, you may write in terms of broad assertions or generalities. For instance, it is better to say, "With your help, we can make Loyalty Sunday a success," rather than, "With your participation we can accelerate the march of Christianity." So stick to specifics. Promise benefits. Be enthusiastic! Keep your letters believable. Then you can move people to action.

9

MAKING
the most of requests

One thing is certain in your ministry: You will receive many kinds of requests and inquiries.

Public relations-wise, you should anticipate as many as possible so that you can (a) answer them promptly, (b) show that you appreciate the opportunity to help, (c) try to help the person even though you can't grant the request, and (d) be ready to explain when you must say "No."

To be sure, the request may be ridiculous, impossible. But no matter what the nature of the request may be, see that your reply is tactful and understanding.

One of the greatest weaknesses in church communication today is the astonishing lack of speed and organization in handling requests. Let's remember that each person who makes a request—for information, material, services—is highly motivated. He wants something—he needs something—and he usually wants it in a hurry.

If you are late with an answer, you may antagonize him. Perhaps you wound his pride, because your delay tells him he isn't very important. Or at least he is likely to believe this request didn't seem very important to you.

Most people are sensitive about being turned down. They are also disappointed when their expectations are not fulfilled. But here's what we must remember: Almost every inquiry and request represents an opportunity for you to build good will in your reply.

Each request may be handled in one of three ways. You may grant it (do so with cordiality and enthusiasm). You may delay a decision. Or you must say "No" tactfully.

Even a routine request may be acknowledged in a manner that wins the confidence and friendship of the inquirer. For example, let's say the women's editor of a local paper requests information about your church for a feature story she is writing. Here's the way it might be answered:

Dear Mrs. Jones:

Here's your copy of "The First Fifty Years." [Request answered cordially.]

You'll find this helpful in writing your feature story for the "Gazette" on the history of early-day churches in Waterloo. [Expression of interest.] When you read this fascinating story, which was written by Charlie Miles, you will find stories about pioneer members of special interest. [Special benefits.]

Please let me know if you need additional information. Your interest in the history of Oakwood Hills Presbyterian Church is really appreciated. [Cordial close.]

Sincerely yours,

Here is another example:

Dear Mrs. Currie:

Thank you for your interest in the booklet, "The Power to See It Through," which we sent to all senior high graduates in our church.

Your copy is enclosed and I hope that your niece in Tucson will be inspired by it as much as have been our own young people.

67

"This pamphlet will give my life new power and direction," one of our seniors told me Sunday. I hope it will mean as much to your niece.

Your minister,

Compare those two letters—friendly and courteous—with the following, which grant requests perfunctorily and even grudgingly.

PERFUNCTORY:

Dear Mr. Dowd:

In compliance with your request of March 8, we are sending you under separate cover a copy of the manual, "Keeping Up Class Interest with Visual Aids."

Yours truly,

GRUDGING:

Dear Mr. Larson:

Requests such as yours of October 8 became so numerous that as a measure of economy we had to refuse them. However, we are making an exception in this instance.

A copy of the manual used by the Jolly Elders in their ceramics class is enclosed. I hope it will be of some benefit to you.

Yours truly,

LETTERS EXPLAINING DELAYED ACTION

Sometimes you cannot take definite action upon inquiry or request. Perhaps you would like more time to consider it, or maybe the request involves the expenditure of considerable time before compliance is possible. In this type of letter it is well to (a) acknowledge it as quickly as possible, (b) explain (if you can) reasons for the delay, and (c) indicate approximately how long it will be before you can answer fully.

Dear Lance:

Your letter of January 15 has just arrived, and I was glad to hear that your work is going well in your new assignment.

I shall be happy to send you the material as soon as possible. Doing so will take a little time, however, because we have misplaced our folder containing Loyalty Sunday publications. We are sure that it is here in the office, so we'll start a thorough search.

As soon as I find it, I'll rush it to you.

Cordially yours,

Dear Chet:

Just a short note to tell you that I have received your letter of September 18. May I have a few days to think this over?

You will hear from me within a week, and I hope it will be possible for me to be of help to you in your proposed program.

Sincerely yours,

SAY "NO" WITH A SMILE

Obviously there are times when you must say "No" to members, friends, and others. In business relationships we are told that "the customer is always right." Often he is in error. And that's true of some persons who make requests of you.

69

When should we say "No"? To whom? Under what conditions? For what reasons? Should we make exceptions and grant the request? How shall we phrase the reply?

First of all, your attitude determines everything. If you are indignant, scornful, suspicious, or unhappy and you retain that attitude when writing a letter, then you are certain to offend the recipient.

Instead, when you say "No" make a sandwich the way all expert letter writers do. It works like this: (a) The top layer starts with something pleasing or positive, (b) the middle layer is a filling of the reasons why you must refuse, and (c) the final layer is like the first, something pleasing—perhaps something you will do. The end of your letter is likely to be remembered longest.

Note the following letters of refusal:

Dear Mrs. Bendex:

How thoughtful of you to offer to give your old piano to the church.

As you know, we need another piano so I asked Thomas Brightwell, who does all of the repair work for all of our pianos, to look at yours.

After making an estimate of the cost to make all needed repairs on yours (parts, tuning, refinishing) he said it would total about $387.00. Members of the music committee, after studying the problem, decided that they would rather apply this amount on a new instrument.

With this explanation I know you will understand the committee's decision. But all of us at First Christian Church appreciate your kindness and thoughtfulness.

Your friend and minister,

Dear Mr. Horning:

Your plan of installing church directories in the lobbies of motels, hotels, the waiting rooms of bus stations, and other spots sounds worthwhile; and I'm sure they will be read by many visitors to our city.

As much as we might be interested in your listing, our advertising budget for the year does not allocate any funds for specialty advertising. All of our money for this purpose is spent for newspaper advertising because of its great impact on hundreds of persons of all ages.

Best of luck to you in your project.

Cordially yours,

Dear Fred:

Your presentation was well done and very favorably received by the board of trustees. I am sorry to report, however, that after considerable deliberation another company was selected.

It should be a source of satisfaction to know that yours was the second choice out of nine presentations.

In about six months we'll have another project, so I'll get in touch with you in plenty of time for you to prepare your presentation.

Sincerely yours,

How very thoughtful,
Mr. Josserand,

of you to write me as you did regarding my sermon, "How to Master Your Moods" which I gave in the series at the First Baptist Church in Charlotte last week.

71

Your request for a copy of my sermon gives me somewhat of a problem because, as you probably noticed, I don't speak from prepared notes. However, I am enclosing a brief outline which will give some of the major points of the sermon.

Also enclosed, Mr. Josserand, is a bibliography. You will find the three books which I have starred helpful and interesting. Thank you so much for making my stay in Charlotte such a pleasant one. Do drop by the next time you come to Lexington.

Sincerely yours,

Dear Mrs. Rhodes:

Thank you for your very nice letter telling of your plans to visit Europe this summer.

I appreciate your telling us about your plans to take movies of ancient churches, battlefields, and other historic spots, and thank you for offering to show these at the church. Program plans for the church night dinners for next year have not been completed, but I suggest that you get in touch with Willard Hammons, chairman, on your return so that your idea can be considered by his committee.

Best wishes for a most enjoyable summer.

Cordially yours,

Dear Mrs. Massad:

Nothing would please me more than to allow you to borrow the coffee urn in Fellowship Hall for the meeting of the Lake Charles Music Club in your home.

Upon checking with Jim Phillips, educational director, I discovered that the urn was purchased by the Guardians Class and was given to the church with the understanding that its use would be limited to church affairs.

Mr. Phillips heard that the American Legion Auxiliary has an urn which can be rented, so perhaps you'd like to get in touch with them. Mrs. Thomas Tingley is President.

Best wishes for an enjoyable club meeting.

Cordially yours,

Dear Mr. Phelps:

It's wonderful to hear that you and other officers of the Kenton Rose Society will be hosts at the state meeting on April 7 and 8.

As much as we would enjoy your group holding the rose show in the assembly room of the Educational Building, the whole area has been carpeted and we are extremely careful to protect it. Our own church groups, for instance, are not allowed to serve refreshments in this room because of the danger of something being spilled.

Thank you for giving me the opportunity to explain the "why" of our policy in the use of this beautiful room.

All good wishes to you and your committee in playing hosts at the forthcoming meeting.

Sincerely yours,

Dear David:

It's wonderful to know of the many new activities which you and other members of your young people's class are sponsoring to raise money for the building fund.

I appreciate your letter suggesting the possibility of showing the film, "Eternal Glory," at a fund-raising dinner. Since I have never seen the film I checked the rating systems of three national magazines and in each discovered that it is not recommended for family or church groups.

73

I'm sure that Arthur Merrill, a member of our church who is associated with the audio-visual office of the Wichita public schools, will be happy to obtain another film for you.

Your leadership and devotion are greatly appreciated by all of us.

Sincerely yours,

Summing up this chapter let's take a look at the highlights:
1. Try to see the situation from the reader's point of view— why he is making the request.
2. Show that the request or offer was given consideration.
3. If you cannot answer a request promptly then send a brief acknowledgement with a promise of a definite answer soon.
4. Remember that your answer—whether "yes," "no," or "perhaps"—can build good will.
5. Say "No" with care and thoughtfulness.
6. Start out with something the reader will like.
7. Try to explain everything from the standpoint of the reader.
8. End on the upbeat with a pleasant close.

10

HOW TO
capitalize on complaints

No minister can be expected to maintain completely harmonious relationships in all phases of church life. The day will never come when you can operate with perfect efficiency because misunderstandings and dissatisfactions are certain to occur. And most of the time the task of straightening out the inevitable "kinks" falls on your shoulders.

As a pastor you must accept those who differ with you on programs and projects. At times you will want to "strike back." "Yet we ought to remember," John H. Olson writes in *Church Management*, "that Jesus did not slap back. If we are going to strike back at all who differ with us or who honestly oppose us in the interest, as they think, of the welfare of the church, then there will be no gospel coming through us to our people. It may be the thunderings of Sinai, but not the voice of Calvary."

Where do these complaints come from? Many come, of course, from major areas of activities. But as a minister you usually fall heir to the delicate task of answering grievances incurred in many relationships, sometimes far removed from direct activities of your work in the parish.

You are not alone because every parish has its critics. "In almost all churches," observed John Timothy Stone, president of Presbyterian Theological Seminary, "there are those members who for one reason or another are out of sympathy with the church and who do not hesitate to express ill will or grievance when the opportunity affords."

75

You can solve many human complications through personal contacts and by telephone, but you can utilize letters in "pouring oil on troubled waters." What's to be done?

1. Find out what happened. Then answer the complaint as soon as possible. Even if you cannot give a definite decision immediately, write a brief note expressing regret for the cause of the complaint and assuring the person that prompt action will be taken.

2. Say something in the beginning to make the person feel you are really glad to know about the difficulty, thank him for telling you. If you can do what he asks, let him know this immediately.

3. Stress what you can do—not what you can't do. Don't repeat the complaint in detail; it may upset the person all over again. Don't repeat his demand, especially if you can't meet it.

4. Show the reader that you appreciate his point of view. Avoid phrases like, "I am at a loss to know" or "I cannot understand." Also avoid phrases which tend to provoke: "you state," "you claim," "you imply," "you assert," and "your complaint." Words to avoid include failure, fault, delay, demand, neglect, insist, and unavoidable.

5. Don't over apologize. Almost always sincere regret is all the reader expects. An apology, properly made, is likely to appeal to his most reasonable self.

6. Avoid statements which sound condescending or grudging. "Naturally we have no obligation under the circumstances; however . . ." Don't imply that the person is unreasonable. "Of course, you realize that every church makes mistakes, especially one as large as ours." Don't say, "Every member was told at the time . . ."

7. If your decision must be negative, don't hide behind the word "policy." Lay the facts on the table so that the person

can understand why you are refusing. And then pass as soon as possible to ideas more agreeable to the person.

8. Don't say, "It will never happen again." Can you be sure it won't?

9. Whether right or wrong your reader must have first consideration, so the letter should be interpreted from his point of view.

10. Avoid the temptation of replying in the discourteous or sarcastic tone of the letter of complaint. Above all, remain calm and courteous if your letter is to build understanding. "A soft answer turneth away wrath" and "grievous words stir up anger."

11. Work hard for an effective ending. Note the following:

Thanks for putting this problem of yours right where it belongs—in our lap.

Thank you for giving me an opportunity to explain this matter.

We shall be grateful for your understanding, your forgiveness, and your assistance.

It gives us pleasure to help you.

Is there any other way we can be of service?

Now let's look at some letters which embody tactfulness of expression in dealing positively and constructively with situations which are essentially negative:

Dear Mr. and Mrs. Sizemore:

You will never know how embarrassed I was to discover that we had omitted David's name from the list of God and Country Boy Scouts published in last week's church paper.

Every item of copy is edited carefully, and then the proofs are read. While we try to keep mistakes at a minimum, once in a while some seemingly preventable error occurs. When it does, of course, we are anxious to correct it.

Please tell David that we are running a separate story about him in next week's paper. He was really faithful in working off requirements for this honor, and I know you are proud of him.

Cordially yours,

Dear Mrs. Barrowman:

Thank you for your letter of December 15.

We would be delighted to keep the church library open some at night. But a survey made last summer showed that users would be satisfied to keep the same schedule (2 until 5 on Tuesday, Wednesday, Thursday, and Friday and 2 until 3:30 Sunday afternoon.) The Sunday assignment, as you may know, is handled by volunteers.

Even though your duties at the office keep you on the job until after 5 each day during the week, we hope you can drop in on Sunday afternoons and choose the books you wish.

More than forty volumes have been added to the library since December 1. Come by and look them over.

Sincerely yours,

Dear Mrs. Ingle:

Thank you for telling us about your experience when you attended the Family Fellowship dinner at the church Wednesday night.

Actually, about twice as many persons as the committee had planned for came and this caused a minor slowdown in serving from the four tables. But our kitchen crew—composed of members of the Builders' Class—accepted the challenge and came through with plenty of food for everyone.

Next time the calling committee, plus members of the

church staff, will urge advance registrations so that the April dinner will proceed right on schedule.

Your interest in our family night program is appreciated.

Sincerely yours,

Dear Mrs. Thurston:

Is my face red?

After writing you as I did in my letter of March 15 and giving you what I thought to be the correct facts, I am very much embarrassed to note my mistake.

Your report of the Visitation Committee was received March 1. Somehow or other it was filed with a report of the Missions Committee. Yesterday we found it, and I saw at once that you have made a most complete and interesting report. Later I want to talk to you about some of your fine suggestions.

Thank you for calling my attention to this matter.

Cordially yours,

Dear Mrs. Stokesberry:

I agree with you that starting the Sunday morning worship with a choir processional has many advantages. And it does help in getting members of the congregation to join in the hymn singing.

But the processional in our church presents several problems. As you have seen, when our choir comes down the center aisle, quite a jam is created in the narthex at the exact time many people are arriving.

In dropping the former type of processional members of the music committee pointed out that there is a limited number of hymn tunes which are also good marching tunes. In other words, our minister of music and members of the music committee weren't exactly certain just how the choir should march in.

79

Actually, the change we have made in the processional is just an experimental endeavor. We agree with Von Ogden Vogt that worship should be an act, not just a passive acceptance of something, and we want to keep that thought uppermost as we review our situation.

Thank you for giving me an opportunity to explain this situation.

Cordially yours,

Dear Mrs. Maremont:

You had every right to be annoyed when you received two reminders requesting action on your Spring Thank Offering which you paid March 10, and we are sorry indeed that the mistake occurred.

As you probably know, the follow-up was done by volunteers. Soon after the first mailing the chairman had a sudden operation. Another person kindly volunteered; and about the time she started to work, she was called out of town because of the serious illness of her mother. But others are helping, and I am glad to say that everything is now running smoothly again.

Thank you for your letter. We appreciate your reporting to us, with such understanding, a situation which has been puzzling to you.

Most sincerely yours,

Dear Mrs. Bobbs:

The quickest way to get a lot of undivided attention is to make a mistake.

This came home to us last week when only half of the membership of the children's choir was announced in the "Evening News."

We aren't sure just where the mixup took place. But everything is ready for the complete membership of the choir to be announced this week as a part of a news story on the forth-coming concert.

Please tell Susan how much we appreciate her singing in the choir this year, and that we are all looking forward to the concert December 15.

Cordially yours,

Dear Mrs. Lane:

Certainly your mother should have been on the list of persons to whom we administered communion during Holy Week. And we did administer it to others at Valley View Nursing Home.

We know that from time to time we do make mistakes; and if these were not called to our attention, we should not be able to correct them and prevent a recurrence. That is why we appreciate your letter.

You are right about our having a large church with many members. But we shall never be so large that we shall overlook the spiritual needs of you and your devoted mother.

In the future your mother will be given a high priority on our communion visitation list.

Your pastor,

Dear Mr. Ledford:

You were quite right to call our attention to some of the errors which have been appearing in our weekly bulletin.

As you know, copy for the bulletin must be written and edited on Monday and then rushed to the print shop. They set the type and send us proofs Wednesday night. Staff members read the proofs and then return them to the printer before Friday morning.

With two of our staff members on vacation and a big back-log of jobs stacked up at the printers, it is evident that everyone has hurried the process a little more than necessary. But your letter helped us to be more careful in writing, editing, and proofreading the copy.

Thank you for writing.

Yours very sincerely,

Dear Mrs. Baxter:

Yes, you are right.

I know how you and members of the Beacon Class must have felt last Sunday when you discovered that the podium had been taken from your room.

As near as I am able to find out, it had been borrowed by a civic club. Evidently it was taken from the church without permission of any staff member. It was returned Tuesday and is now back in its usual place.

Thank you for calling this to our attention.

Sincerely yours,

(In this type of explanation, no specific reasons can explain the situation. You can only conjecture as to what may have happened. This serves the purpose, however, for it shows that you are concerned about the situation.)

As you see from these examples, it is well to indicate at the very beginning of your letter that you understand the reader's point of view and that you welcome his note. Use a friendly, personal tone, and seek to make him feel that his problem will be given sympathetic treatment. In every instance use persuasion rather than argument. Make every knock a boost. Solve each problem thoughtfully, patiently, and gracefully. Work hard for a positive ending. Finally, remember that "he that ruleth his spirit [is better] than he that taketh a city."

11

BOOSTING
interest in special events

In Grandma's day the church was a place to go mainly for worship. Occasionally members enjoyed church suppers and other functions. But many churches were dark and their doors locked during the week. How different today when the church operates on a seven-day basis.

"We never close" might be the slogan of many churches.

The "new-time" religion includes a variety of events and services within the church: craft classes, recreation facilities, drama groups, Sunday evening clubs, Bible study groups. But many churches also range far beyond their walls with summer caravans for young people, visits to hospitals, services to patients in rest homes, prayer breakfasts in homes, and many other events.

Do we have too many activities? Any strategy you can employ to show people the Christian way of life is all right. I have known skillful people to use the tennis court to the glory of God and the salvation of people.

How can a busy pastor publicize the many varied events and services of his church? He can use the various channels—the church bulletin, news stories in the local newspaper, posters, announcements from the pulpit, the church newspaper, telephone calls, and others. Each is effective in its own way.

But he should make use of effective letters—letters sent to individuals and mass mailings. No matter how large the congregation each member can be reached as an individual by letter.

Any other special advantages? Yes. You can (a) extend personal invitations to special groups and individuals, (b) pre-check possible attendance, (c) "humanize" your church by using a personalized approach, and (d) build interest and attendance in any event or service, large or small.

Note the following examples:

"Guidebook to Better Teaching"
"Creeds of the Churches"
"How to Publicize Church Activities"
"Jesus' Teachings for Young People"
"Children's Sermonettes"

You've probably guessed it.

These are just a few titles from more than one hundred books which have been added to the church library since October 15.

You'll find an amazing variety of books—drama, biography, self-help, reference, historical, current affairs, music—and many others.

We're delighted that our library, which really didn't get started until five years ago, now boasts more than seventeen hundred books. In addition, it now receives fourteen periodicals for the use of our members.

"I had no idea what a marvelous library our church had until recently," a new member told me. Then he continued, "No matter what your age or interests, I am convinced that one visit to the library on the second floor of the Educational Building will make you a regular reader."

Is that you heading for the library?

Cordially yours,

A word to the wise . . .

You are cordially invited to see the filmstrip, "Apostle to the Indians," just released by the American Bible Society, at the annual dinner for Sunday school teachers and staff members at the church at 6:30 Thursday night, April 24.

You'll enjoy this filmstrip which describes John Eliot's work with the Massachusetts Indians and the translation of the first Bible in North America into the language of these Indians. It also shows Eliot's dedication and perseverance in converting the Indians and how he overcame the difficulties of learning their language and translating the Bible so they might read and understand.

Do plan to see this inspiring presentation. For reservations call Mrs. Stubler at the church office (JE 4-7654) before Tuesday.

Your pastor,

Did you hear about

the kid who was asked by the teacher, "Now, Bobby, tell me where elephants are found?" and he replied, "Elephants are so big that they're hardly ever lost."

Maybe not elephants but smaller things are often misplaced—things like gloves, coats, galoshes, mufflers, rain coats, and hats.

Have you or your children left anything at church lately? Maybe you've misplaced something and forgotten where you left it. There is a chance that you may have left it at church and it may be in the many items now found in the Lost and Found shelves of the church office.

Call Mrs. Eckler (PE 4-7435) or, better still, drop by the church office and check over the articles. Whatever you've lost just might be there.

Your minister,

You'll get
a big lift,

when you hear the a cappella choir of Concordia College present a concert of seasonal religious music at 8 p.m. Monday, March 22, at Grace Lutheran Church.

Works of such master composers as Bach, Brahms, and Gesius, as well as those of contemporary composers, Bender and Lenel, will be sung by the choir, consisting of preministerial and teacher-training students.

"An unforgettable experience!" was the enthusiastic comment of a listener after last year's concert. Come and bring your friends Monday night and you'll agree with him.

Cordially yours,

Yes, Mr. Basset,
we're going to

hold a reservation for you. But the way reservations are coming in for the lecture by Dr. Samuel Dombeck for the spring dinner of the Men's Club on April 28, it won't be long before all tickets will be sold.

After Dr. Dombeck's appearance in Seattle here's how a reporter summarized his lecture: "Dr. Dombeck is a versatile interpreter of life and living. He gave all who heard him a joyously rewarding evening."

So—now before you forget—call the church office (EX 4-6754) for your reservation!

Cordially yours,

Dear Friend:

You don't have to be a theologian to know—

—how the Bible was written.

—why it remains the world's leading best-seller.

—what its message is for the world today.

No, you don't have to be a graduate of a theological seminary to appreciate the values of the Bible. You can do it easily by attending the Sunday evening sessions which will be taught by Dr. Robert Scott, our associate pastor.

When? Seven Sunday evenings (6 until 7) beginning next Sunday, October 12—Beacon Classroom.

Typical of many fine comments following this series last year was the statement of Mrs. Howard Benson: "This was one of the greatest thrills of my church life." So bring your Bible and come—and you'll be thrilled, too!

Your minister,

Dear Friends:

When you come to church next Sunday, you will take part in dedication ceremonies for the new cross on the communion table. As we look at the symbol of Christianity, let's remind ourselves

that the cross—

is symbolic of obedience, for our Lord was obedient "unto death, even death on a cross."

is symbolic of God's attractiveness to man. Jesus stated it beautifully, "And I, when I am lifted up from the earth, will draw all men to myself."

is symbolic of victory.

is a symbol of glory. With Paul we may learn to glory not in our own background of experience but in the cross of Christ.

The more we meditate on the cross the better we understand all that John Bowring implied when he wrote:

"In the cross of Christ I glory,
Towering o'er the wrecks of time;
All the light of sacred story
Gathers 'round its head sublime."

87

So as we dedicate the cross Sunday, let's remind ourselves that it is a symbol of Christianity, of God's love for sinful man, and of triumphant hope.

Your minister,[1]

Dear Friend:

A man's brain is a strange mechanism. It starts working the minute we are born and quits the moment we get up to make a speech.

But we've solved the problem. Beginning next Tuesday night at 7 o'clock we are starting a class in public speaking. John Patterson, one of our members who is a speech teacher at Lexington High School, will serve as instructor for the six-weeks course.

Something else: John won't try to make orators of everyone. Rather he will show us how to meet typical speech situations with confidence.

This idea came from officers of the Builders' Class which is sending ten enrollees. Only thirty-five persons can be accommodated in the Wesley Room where sessions will be held each Tuesday evening from 7 until 9.

Interested? Then call Miss Meadows at the church office (WA 4-5643). First come, first served!

Cordially yours,

(This letter was sent to Sunday school teachers.)

This letter,
Mrs. Collins,

—contains both a "thank you" and an invitation!

First, we are grateful to you for serving as an officer in the Woman's Society of Christian Service during the past year. This is greatly appreciated.

[1] Adapted from "The Symbolism of the Cross" by Friedrich Rest, *Church Management*, February, 1958, pp. 16-17.

Second, we'd like to urge you to attend the district training school in Tulsa, September 5. Mrs. J. H. Prentice of the St. Louis Council of Churches will serve as director. You've read her monthly column, "Living Faith," in "The Church Woman."

You'll find a complete program for the day, a reservation card, and a self-addressed envelope enclosed. May we hear from you?

Cordially yours,

Dear Mrs. Jennings:

Looking for literature which explains the church to teenagers?

Then look no more, Mrs. Jennings, because our church library has just received twenty-three books on church history, traditions, and beliefs. You'll find the titles, authors, and brief descriptions of the books on the attached sheet.

As you know, books may be checked out during the following hours: 2 until 5 p.m. (Monday through Friday), 8 until 12 Saturday morning, and 4 until 6 Sunday afternoons.

Stop in soon and look over the new books.

Sincerely yours,

Dear Friends:

Memorial Drive Church is a big church with lots of people. But somehow certain folks stand out even in the crowd. We can't invite everyone to our "old-fashioned church picnic" but we sure would like to have you come.

If you like fun, if you like people, if you like to laugh, you'll love our church picnic. Every year it is one of the real highlights of our congregation's life, and we know you'll enjoy it.

Time—This Sunday, July 12, 4:00 to 8:00 p.m.

We thought this would give you an excellent opportunity also to meet our folks on an informal basis. Naturally we think they are "the greatest" and we know you would like them and vice-versa.

Come if you possibly can. A list of what to bring is printed below.

If ever we can be of any help to you be sure to call us.

Sincerely,

A, B, C—Relishes (Pickles, Olives, etc.)
D through J—Salads (vegetable or fruit—no molded)
K through Z—Fried Chicken
please bring 3 times what your family eats in relishes and
   salads, 2 times for chicken.

THANKS FOR YOUR HELP!   HOPE TO SEE YOU THERE! [2]

I WISH YOU COULD HAVE BEEN
THERE WITH ME—

That was a moment to remember and a sight to see—the full moon coming up on Lake Texoma, the waves gently lapping the shore, men singing the old hymns around a dying campfire. And the sincere testimonials of men telling how Christ has been their partner in life.

I wish I could put into words all that I saw and felt there— there in the fall retreat for the men of our church.

You know what I mean if you've ever been there. You'll want to go back this year.

Never been? Then you'll want to enjoy the Christian fellowship, the food, and the fun of the men's fall retreat at the

---

[2] This letter, sent to group of best prospects, gets terrific results. Used by Charlie Shedd and Jim Brock, ministers at Memorial Drive Presbyterian Church, Houston, Tex.

lake camp Friday night through Saturday afternoon, October 25-26.

Read the enclosed program and then call Bob Sears (JA 5-5643 office) for a reservation. Call him today!

Sincerely yours,

Dear Mr. Kidd:

"One of the biggest troubles with success is that its recipe is often the same as that for a nervous breakdown."

That's a quotation from "Tapping Your Hidden Powers," written by Arthur B. Whittlesey, author and traveler, who will address the Men's Club at the installation dinner in the church dining room at 6:30 Tuesday night, April 22.

You'll enjoy hearing him, I'm sure, so make your reservation by calling Mrs. Newcomb (SU 5-6543) today!

Sincerely yours,

43 . . . 72 . . . 65 . . . 89

Yes, Mr. Harrison, the quarterback is calling your signal— inviting you and yours to attend the annual Father-Son banquet in the church dining room at 6 o'clock Thursday evening, December 10.

W. H. "Bear" Baker, who coached the Middlevale University Leopards to forty-three consecutive victories, will discuss, "Scouting the Game of Life." Mr. Baker is an active member of the First Baptist Church at Norfolk and is in great demand as a speaker at youth meetings.

We know that the evening planned for you and yours, Mr. Harrison, will score a touchdown in both enjoyment and entertainment.

For reservations (plates are $1.50) call Miss Kramer at MU 3-5643 today!

Sincerely yours,

EXPRESSING THANKS FOR HELP

Mrs. Butterworth

this is just

a note to

T ell you
H ow sincerely we
A ppreciate your help at the opening of our
N ew Educational Building. We are deeply grateful, and
K now that your services helped to make the occasion a
big success.

Y ou can be sure that all of
O ur members and staff appreciate your
U nselfish efforts in making the occasion such a glorious
one.

EXPLAINING DELAY IN NEW PROGRAM

Dear Mr. Wilmot:

"Why hasn't the new recreation hall opened?"

You've probably asked that question. And so have hundreds of others. And it's a natural question because we had hoped to open the new hall about March 10.

First of all, the rains came—and kept coming. Naturally, so much wet weather threw the contractor behind schedule. Then several shipments of steel beams were delayed. Shipments of other material arrived behind schedule. And then, just as we were making fair progress, we were notified of a shutdown at the brick plant.

Reason enough? But I'm glad to tell you that the finishing touches are now being applied and we hope to open the plant May 24.

Just wait until you see it and you'll agree that it was certainly worth waiting for!

Cordially yours,

As you see from these examples, a letter promoting a special event or service often permits you greater flexibility in copy tone and layout. What's more, you may wish to use gay colors in some of your mailings. Above all, see that your letter stands out; see that it attracts and holds the reader's attention. Then your message will be read and remembered—and people will respond!

12

FRIENDLY
notes that get results

If anyone needs a multiple personality, it is the minister. No matter how much theological training he receives, he cannot be fully prepared for the avalanche of demands he must face when he becomes pastor of a church.

He is expected to be scholar, group therapist, marriage counselor, administrator, civic leader, fund raiser, bookkeeper, public relations expert, scoutmaster, diplomat, psychoanalyst, mimeograph machine technician, chamber of commerce speaker, and even janitor and plumber.

That isn't all. He must visit the sick, the aged, and newcomers. And, just as important, he must call on backsliders and church members who make demands on his time. Somehow he must take time each day for study, personal prayer, and reading. At the end of the day he may grab a few minutes to be with his family before returning to the church for a committee meeting, a men's social, a youth group, or counseling which may keep a family from falling apart.

And he may admit, "I just don't have time to keep up with my personal correspondence." By the time he fulfills his many roles—well, there just aren't enough hours in the day.

One thing is certain: The busier he is, the more he should take advantage of letters to cement relationships and build good will. He will find that his messages will show returns immeasurably greater than the small amount of time required to write them. Letters can reach people as individuals, save time, and win new friends for any church. Take a typical day:

John Dermott, one of your members, has applied for another position and would like a letter of recommendation.

Mrs. Pat Hoyt's mother died in Arizona and you want to send condolences.

You are invited to serve on the Red Cross board but feel that you must decline.

Suddenly you remember that the tentative program of the visitation campaign submitted by Frank Harris was never acknowledged.

Recommending a member, extending condolences, declining an appointment, apologizing for late acknowledgment of report—these are just a few of the ways that friendly letters can solve routine situations and retain the good will of others.

"Letter writing has always played a very important part in my ministry," R. Paul Caudill, pastor of the First Baptist Church, Memphis, Tennessee, says. "The written word will often accomplish more than the spoken word. One can look upon the written word again and again. The spoken word often dies upon the ear.

"A letter reflects the character of the writer. Its clarity of expression, its piquancy, its gentleness, its modesty, its careful choice of words, its delicate nuances of thought all together serve to present an image of the man who wrote it."

Yes, a letter is a unique form of communication and as such has a power and influence of its own. Not just any kind of letter, to be sure, but one which is planned and written for a specific purpose. You can get along in your ministry with little letter writing. But what dividends in good will and cooperation come from a human and dynamic letter program! Here are a number of effective examples.

95

LETTERS OF INTRODUCTION

Dear Gilbert:

My good friend, James Dillion, will present this note to you when he stops in Louisville on his way to New York.

James is writing an article showing how large department stores are stepping up their community relations. He knows that by talking to you he can obtain information about your excellent program at Ryerson and Son.

Since you are an authority in this particular area, he has asked for an introduction to you. I shall appreciate any courtesies you may show him.

Cordially yours,

Dear Bruce:

My friend, Roy Donnelley, of whom you have heard me speak, will be spending the weekend of September 17-18 in St. Louis, making his headquarters at Hotel Jefferson.

Roy is greatly interested in motivation research in advertising, and knowing your interest in this subject makes me think you will find him most congenial. You are unusually busy at this time of year, I know, but if you have a little free time during Roy's visit, I am sure both of you would enjoy getting together.

Sincerely yours,

LETTERS OF DECLINATION

Letters of declination work best when you combine cordiality with tact. Above all, you should always explain the circumstances which prevent acceptance. The letter is strengthened when you express appreciation for the invitation. Summing up: The letter must be written in a tone which convinces its recipient that you were pleased to receive the invitation and that you regret that other commitments or obligations prevent your acceptance.

Dear Mr. Durland:

Please accept my sincere thanks for your letter of October 17, inviting me to serve as a member of the Bordentown Park Board.

Certainly your group has accomplished wonders in expanding our park program to meet the needs of hundreds each summer.

As much as I would enjoy helping, I am serving this year on two conference committees of the church (with state-wide responsibilities) and besides I am trying to complete a book manuscript.

I want you and your fellow board members to know, however, that I feel highly complimented at your invitation, and that I am most appreciative of it.

Cordially yours,

Dear Mr. Westrick:

I consider it a high compliment to be invited to join the Civic Betterment League of Covington. Thank you sincerely for your letter.

Just now, however, we are holding our Sunday school leadership classes on Tuesday night, so I could not attend any of the League meetings.

Please express my appreciation to members of your group for all that they are doing to make Covington a more desirable city. And convey my deep appreciation to members of the League for extending me an invitation to join.

Very sincerely yours,

Dear Mr. Wampler:

It would be a pleasure to become associated with your splendid organization, and I sincerely appreciate your courtesy in inviting me.

Just now I am giving all possible time and effort in completing the financial campaign for our new sanctuary. As you know, this involves many hours of planning and counseling with many committees in addition to my usual duties as minister.

Obviously, therefore, it would be impossible for me to attend meetings of your group with any regularity.

I want you and your fellow members to know, however, that I feel highly complimented at your invitation, and that I am most appreciative of it.

Cordially yours,

Dear Homer:

Thank you for your gracious letter of March 25.

Nothing would please me more than to have the privilege of giving the baccalaureate sermon to members of the senior class of Kirkwood High School on June 2.

As much as I would enjoy doing this, a quick look at my calendar shows that I have a previous engagement in Joplin that night.

You have a fine group of seniors, I know, and I wish that circumstances permitted my acceptance. I thank you most sincerely for your invitation.

Cordially yours,

Dear Ronald:

I would consider it a great honor to address the Scottish Rite club at its monthly dinner on September 25.

Unfortunately, however, we are sponsoring a missions school for all churches of the district that week with our church staff and board serving as hosts.

It was fine of you to invite me, and if your program schedule should work out so you could give me another chance in the months ahead, I'll do my best to come.

Sincerely yours,

Dear Mrs. Doke:

Thank you for your letter of February 15, in which you invite me to serve as judge in the high school essay contest with the topic, "America's Responsibility in Today's World."

I should like very much to serve in this capacity. Recently, however, in losing one staff member and training another, my work has materially increased. And I feel it would be unfair to accept a task in which I cannot give the proper amount of time.

Nevertheless, I want you to know that your invitation is much appreciated, and that you have my best wishes in this worthwhile program.

Cordially yours,

Dear Don:

Your cordial invitation for me to give the invocation at the "N" Club dinner at Norman High School on Thursday night, April 25, is greatly appreciated.

As much as I would like to accept, a quick glance at my calendar shows that I am to attend Pastors' Week at Southern Methodist University from April 21 to April 26.

All of us are proud of the fine records made by all teams of Norman High this year, and I think you and your fellow officers should be congratulated for sponsoring this recognition dinner.

Do let me know if I can be of help on future occasions.

Sincerely yours,

LETTERS OF RECOMMENDATION

Every letter of recommendation should pinpoint specific characteristics of the person, not just his competence as a specific kind of worker but relevant personal characteristics. The mere assertion that "he is one of the most outstanding young men of the community" is too vague. Rather it is always better to give specific details.

One thing is certain: The tone of enthusiasm adds to the favorable effect of the message. Give proof of characteristics when possible. Example: Instead of stating that a young person is a leader, show the specific offices he has held which indicate that he is a leader.

Here are some representative specimens:

Dear Mrs. Ingram:

I am very glad to answer your inquiry of April 22 about the qualifications of Phyllis Clymer as camp counselor.

Miss Clymer was employed for two summers to set up two of our junior high camps. During both summers her work was more than satisfactory—it was excellent. She is an expert swimmer, excellent in human relations, and is really motivated to work with youngsters. She is mature in her judgment, enthusiastic, and is most dependable.

She is responsible, careful in following instructions, and is well liked by all (parents, youngsters, and staff). She is neat and attractive in appearance.

I feel that you would be fortunate in securing Miss Clymer's services as a counselor, and I recommend her without reservation.

Sincerely yours,

Dear Mr. Eastman:

Efficiency, honesty, friendliness, enthusiasm—these are the qualities that first occur to me in describing Jerry Dunn, about whom you inquire in your letter of May 19.

Jerry served as custodian for us for three years, and I found him highly cooperative, energetic, and painstaking. So many people said, "We've lost the best one we've ever had," when he left the church staff to work at Hall Brothers.

In my close association with him I have been impressed with his ambition, his integrity, and his desire to make the most of every situation. I feel that his services would be a definite asset to your organization.

Yours sincerely,

Dear Dwight:

If it happens that you could use a good secretary on your staff, you'll welcome the news that Pam Resler—the best secretary I've had in years—is about to leave me.

Her family is moving to St. Paul about June 1, and she feels she should go along.

Maybe I am going overboard, Dwight, but I can't speak highly enough of her. She's a marvelous typist. She anticipates every need. She's thoroughly dependable in every way. And equally important, she gets along fine with everybody.

Let me know promptly if you're at all interested. I don't believe she'll be available long.

Cordially yours,

Dear Mr. Bastron:

This is a letter I am happy to write, for I can recommend Ruth Garwin wholeheartedly for the position as staff writer in the news bureau of Middlevale College.

101

I have known Miss Garwin for more than eight years. As a reporter for the "Daily News" she wrote an amazing number of feature stories which received high recognition in contests sponsored by the Indiana Press Association.

As you probably know, she was a staff assistant in the news bureau during her undergraduate day at Southeastern. She served as editor of the college newspaper and as a senior received the Golden "S" which goes to the most outstanding student in journalism.

Miss Garwin is enthusiastic, tactful, and energetic. I have come to admire in her the qualities of sound judgment, analytical mind, and devotion to the job at hand. I am sure that any responsibility you may entrust to her will be diligently fulfilled.

Very sincerely yours,

Dear Mr. Finley:

I am delighted to recommend George Dobry, whom I have known for ten years.

Mr. Dobry is an extremely intelligent, capable man. In my personal association with him on several community projects, I have found him to be a very capable organizer and to be unusually successful in working with others.

It is significant that he has served as District Governor of Rotary Clubs, a member of the Board of Education, and as a member of the city park board. Here at Nichols Hills Christian Church he has taught a men's Sunday school class which has shown a constant growth under his leadership.

My recommendation of Mr. Dobry, therefore, is made without reservation. Everything I know about him is to his credit.

Cordially yours,

Dear Dean Mason:

Of the hundreds of young men whom I have known in several pastorates, Burleigh Smith, who plans to attend the University of Arizona, is one of the most outstanding.

Burleigh has served as president of the Student Council at Kilgore High School, was elected a delegate to Boys State, and is a member of the National Honor Society. Furthermore, he has made the honor roll each term which is noteworthy when you consider that he has worked after school and on Saturdays as a checker at a supermarket.

In serving as president of the youth group at our church he not only set an example of the best in Christian living, but he sparked all members with high ideals and enthusiasm.

He is friendly, conscientious, dependable.

Summing up: He is tops in every way.

Sincerely yours,

LETTERS OF APOLOGY

Sooner or later a situation arises which calls for a note of apology. Whether the cause is forgetfulness, a heavy schedule, or procrastination, a sincere letter of apology will build understanding. Explain the "why" of the delay if you have an adequate reason. If none exists, a frank admission of the fact usually has a disarming effect upon the reader.

EXPLAINING DELAY IN RETURNING BORROWED PROPERTY

Dear Martin:

In returning your book, "Beyond Conformity," I want to express to you both my thanks and my apologies.

Actually I have had this book so long that I'm embarrassed, but my reading has been interrupted so much lately in pushing plans for our church expansion.

It was generous of you to share this stimulating volume with me, and I do hope you have not been inconvenienced by the delay in its return.

Sincerely yours,

Dear Eddie:

It was mighty fine of you to let me borrow your book, "How to Use Tact and Skill in Handling People," and I am ashamed to be so slow in returning it.

Many of the ideas discussed will be of great worth to me in my ministry. Please accept both my thanks for your generosity and my sincere apology for having kept it so long.

Cordially yours,

EXPLAINING DELAY IN ACKNOWLEDGING FAVOR OR COURTESY

Dear Mr. Sickels:

For weeks I have intended to thank you for your kindness in writing Guy Barrett about my stay in Atlanta. Meeting him was a most enjoyable experience, and he certainly did a lot to make my stay such a pleasant one.

One afternoon he drove me on a tour of some of the historic sites near the city and then took me to his home for dinner that night.

I appreciate the thoughtful courtesy on your part far more than the date of this letter might indicate.

Sincerely yours,

Dear Mrs. Hinman:

I'm ashamed to think how long it has been since you sent me your suggestions for next summer's Vacation Bible School. I had intended to read them and then write you about them, but two out-of-town evangelistic campaigns prevented my doing so until a few days ago.

You have done a remarkably fine job of analyzing the many factors which contribute to a successful vacation school. Your suggestions for strengthening the areas of staff recruitment and promotion are both practical and unique.

You devoted a lot of time to this analysis, I know, and I do appreciate all of the hard work and thought which went into your recommendations. Despite this long-delayed acknowledgment, I do appreciate your many fine suggestions. Copies of your report will be mailed to members of the Board of Education for further consideration.

Sincerely yours,

Dear Dave:

I have long intended to thank you for sending me Dale Harper's article, "The New Time Religion," in "Church News" for September.

I profited greatly from reading it, and if it hadn't been for you the chances are that I would not have seen it.

Please accept my apology for this belated expression of thanks. It was thoughtful of you to send it because it is certainly most worthwhile.

Cordially yours,

EXPLAINING DELAYED ACTION

Dear Mr. Van Ness:

Your letter of April 25 has been read with much interest.

Your proposal of rotating membership on the Board of Stewards has been discussed at several meetings through the years but no specific action has ever been taken. Certainly the plan has several advantages.

I'm leaving tonight for a ministers' conference in Kansas City, and I shall be away from the office for four or five days. As soon as I return, I shall get in touch with you so that we can discuss your suggestions.

Very sincerely yours,

Dear Mrs. Barr:

Your letter of March 23 has just arrived, and I appreciate your suggestions to raise funds to redecorate the nursery.

Members of the Board of Trustees are discussing several "must" repair and redecorating jobs. They will decide which ones have priority at their meeting April 5. I shall be glad to get in touch with you following their meeting.

Thank you for your interest in this worthwhile project.

Sincerely yours,

LATE ACKNOWLEDGMENT OF COMMITTEE REPORT

Dear Mr. Kraft:

I have long intended to express my appreciation to you and other members of your committee for the excellent report which you submitted on improved ways of expanding our visitation program.

In reading the news story of the district training school for visitation workers to be held in St. Paul, I suddenly remembered that the report of your committee had not been acknowledged.

I was especially interested in your findings that we are reaching only about one third of the newcomers to our city, and your excellent suggestions of contacting these folk soon after they move here.

Despite this long-delayed acknowledgment I do appreciate the splendid work by you and your committee. I have read the report with much interest. Your committee had done a remarkably fine job; in fact, the report is one of the most complete and comprehensive that I have ever seen.

Please accept my sincere thanks for your fine work.

Cordially yours,

REQUESTING INFORMATION

Dear Ernest:

Would you do something for me?

It shouldn't take you but a few minutes for you probably have the information I want right at your fingertips.

What I need is the name and address of a good organ repairman—someone who is an expert in doing a complete "tune-up" job on a large instrument.

You've used several so I know that you can suggest the right person. Many thanks for your help.

Cordially yours,

"THANK-YOU" TO GUEST SPEAKERS

Dear Mr. Lesley:

"Most worthwhile!"

That comment voiced by a longtime member of our church summarized the reaction of many others who enjoyed your sparkling address at our recent church night dinner.

With the inspirational boost which we all received from your address on "The Power of Personal Influence" I'm sure that our church will attain new goals in stewardship and giving during the year ahead.

Thank you again for the tremendous lift which you gave us.

Cordially yours,

Dear Mr. Trimble:

I want to thank you again for the stirring message on "The Perils of Pornography" which you presented to our youth group at its meeting Sunday night.

No program in months has met such an attentive reception or produced so much enthusiastic comment on the part of our youngsters.

I feel that it was a real privilege to hear you speak, and I thank you for giving us such a timely and outstanding program.

Sincerely yours,

INVITATION TO SPEAKER

Dear Mr. Donahue:

I've heard so many good things about the talk you made at the District Rotary Conference last week that I'd be delighted if you could give it at the fall dinner of the men's club of Trinity Episcopal Church either November 14 or 21.

The subject of mental health for business and professional men would certainly interest all members of our group, and I know you would receive a great response.

If you can be with us on either of these dates, I'll announce the good news in our parish newsletter, and we'll have a peak attendance for your appearance.

Cordially yours,

Really there's no limit to the uses of the personal letter in strengthening friendships and building church loyalty. Every day brings opportunities for you to show others that you are thoughtful, gracious, and prompt in your friendly relations. Put more good-will letters to work for you!

13

BUILDING UP
your community image

Yesterday's parson knew and was known by everyone in the community. He and his family were frequent dinner guests in the homes of members of his congregation. He studied, prayed, prepared sermons, and called on church members during the week. Each Sunday he preached two sermons. He was intimately associated with community life.

How different today when the minister faces enough demands in one day to exhaust the average man. On every hand he finds that a myriad of community enterprises request the help and guidance of the professional servant of God.

One thing is certain: If the many and varied services of the modern church are to be successful, they must first be assured of a happy reception by the community of which they are a part. And interestingly enough what the public thinks of you and your church—rather than what you think of it—gauges the success or failure of your enterprise.

Community acceptance is vital to the success of your ministry. At times this reaction is separate from your power in the pulpit. Lewis M. Blackmer, Jr., once told of a minister whose people sometimes wondered if he had prepared his sermon. "When he spoke, they say, his voice was high and strong—hard to listen to for any length of time," Mr. Blackmer wrote in *Church Management*. "Yet he did a marvelous work for the Master, the church, the community, and the state, and his memory will outlast that of many who have stood among the best of preachers."

By maintaining a harmonious relationship with community leaders and groups—those who are vital in creating and molding public opinion in your city—you can strengthen the collective opinion regarding you and your church.

As a minister you have a goal and a vision for your people and the community. Mark Rich once pointed out in the *Pulpit*:

He (the minister) has a holy dissatisfaction with some aspects of individual and community life. Thus he is always living in two worlds; the community that is and the one that is to be . . . He is like the wise man who saw a vision and followed it. He is on his way. He not only looks forward to the coming of the kingdom but is taking steps to bring it into fulfillment in his community.

At best you cannot join with each and every one of the numerous social-interest groups so characteristic of our culture. Rather you have found that you should participate in as many community-betterment programs as time permits, and then maintain friendly relations with leaders in other areas of civic improvement.

Many of the potential courtesies of community relationships are splendidly adapted to expression through personal letters. A few words of appreciation for the kindness of a friend, a congratulatory note to a person who has received a promotion, a word of encouragement to a high school student, a thoughtful note to a person upon retirement—all these are opportunities for thoughtfulness.

Where do you get ideas for these letters? Your best source is your local newspaper. But you should also be on the alert for letter ideas in conversation, telephone calls, conferences, home visits, civic meetings, staff meetings, and your other contacts.

Keep up as many community contacts as possible. In addition, you can "multiply yourself" and also instill a genuine sense of appreciation and worth of yourself and your church through friendly letters to community leaders and others performing noteworthy services.

UPON PROFESSIONAL OR CIVIC HONOR

Dear Mr. Whitaker:

This is just a word to tell you how glad I was to learn that you have been selected Chairman of the Cleveland County Chapter of the American Red Cross.

Like a true friend in need, Red Cross comes to the aid of many in peace and in war, in disaster and in sickness. As the Red Cross expands to meet the increasing needs for its services to American families, it will need leaders like you to meet the larger work load of its volunteers.

Your election is the best possible recognition of long and efficient service to this great organization. I am happy for you in your success.

Sincerely yours,

UPON ELECTION

Dear Mr. Harper:

I feel that all of us in Middletown can be very proud of your election as President of the New Mexico Education Association.

All of us here certainly appreciate the fine way in which you are serving as Superintendent of Schools, particularly in directing the expansion program.

You are to be congratulated upon this recognition of your high standing among the educators of the state.

Sincerely yours,

Dear Leslie:

As I browsed through the Sunday "Gazette," my eyes fell on an item headed: "Parker New Head of Rotarians."

Your election to the presidency of this dynamic organization is splendid recognition of your ability. In working with you I have discovered that you have no small enthusiasms, and I know that Rotarians will profit greatly from your leadership and organizational ability.

Congratulations and more power to you!

Cordially yours,

Dear Mr. Maguire:

CONGRATULATIONS!!!

May I add my felicitations to the many you have already received for the high recognition which came to the Middlevale High School at the National Band Clinic in Chicago.

Many honors have come to the group since you became director eight years ago, and I know that everyone in the community will share my feeling of satisfaction that you and your young musicians have brought this new recognition to our city.

All good wishes to you in continuing your splendid work.

Sincerely yours,

Dear Mr. Scribner:

Warmest congratulations to you upon being chosen "Citizen of the Year" by the Cedarvale Chamber of Commerce!

In reading the list of your various services to so many groups through the years—school board, church, park board, Kiwanis Club, Retail Merchants' Association, Campfire Girls, and others—I am convinced that by every standard of measurement you have earned this high honor.

Your fine example will inspire all of us to do more for Cedarvale.

Cordially yours,

Dear Mr. Brownell:

Just a few words to tell you how glad I was to read in the morning paper that you have been named chairman of the Community Chest.

Your appointment is the best possible recognition of long and unselfish service to the community. I am happy for you in your new honor.

Cordially yours,

Dear Dwight:

I was delighted to learn of your election as president of the Springdale Chamber of Commerce and I am sure my reaction is typical of everyone in the community.

You have earned this honor through years of unselfish work in many areas of civic service, and you are eminently qualified to fulfill the responsibility which it carries.

Let me know if I can help you and other officers in realizing the organization's motto, "Meeting the Challenge," in the year ahead.

Congratulations and best wishes for success!

Cordially yours,

Dear Alexander:

This is just a note to congratulate you upon your election as chairman of the Grant Park Library Board.

113

I'm inclined to agree with Voltaire who wrote many years ago, "All the known world, excepting only savage nations, is governed by books."

Yes, they do play a tremendous role in our lives, and that's why I'm so delighted that you are going to extend the influence of books in our community.

Best wishes.

Sincerely yours,

UPON OUTSTANDING COMMUNITY SERVICE

Dear Mr. Griswold:

This is just a little note to tell you how much we appreciate Channel 4 carrying the Sunday afternoon program, "Know Your Bible."

You are aware of the fact that this informative program attracts many viewers, mainly because of the high competence of the religious leaders who serve on the weekly panel.

You have the gratitude of officials and members of many churches, but also that of many other persons who are interested in hearing various interpretations of biblical passages.

Yours very truly,

Dear Mrs. Dobbins:

Heartiest congratulations on the interesting display of old family Bibles which you featured as one of your exhibits at the city library during American Library Week.

These old books not only brought back memories to oldtimers, but they also fascinated many youngsters of today.

You are doing an exceptionally fine job as librarian, and I want to congratulate you and your staff for providing all of us in Park Ridge with such an outstanding service.

Cordially yours,

Dear Mr. Poynor:

Heartiest congratulations to you and other members of the Middletown Junior Chamber of Commerce for sponsoring the annual toy drive again this year.

From past years I know how many hundreds of youngsters are thrilled by the coming of Christmas because of the worthwhile project which the Jaycees sponsor.

You and your fellow members will enjoy a happier Christmas because you give so much and in turn you experience that great joy which comes from helping others.

Cordially yours,

UPON SPECIAL SERVICE OR ACHIEVEMENT

Dear Clayton:

Years ago I had a friend in St. Louis who once remarked, "When you're pushing sixty that's exercise enough."

But that isn't quite enough, so that's why I am so happy about your sparking the South Bend recreation committee in its efforts to see that more people of all ages take part in some kind of sports or vigorous recreation.

In our modern technological society man is no longer required to move vigorously in meeting his daily needs. It's mighty easy to be afflicted with "spectatoritis."

You and other members of your committee can do a world of good in showing more persons how physical fitness can add to their health and pleasure.

Congratulations on your most worthwhile efforts!

Cordially yours,

Dear Chief McGraw:

This is just a brief note to thank you and members of the Lake View police force for providing police escorts for funeral processions.

115

So often I have heard other ministers and also members of families concerned tell how much the services of your force mean to them. Your help means more since the great increase of traffic in our city.

All of us are grateful to you and your men for this service.

Sincerely yours,

Dear Donald Lane:

Heartiest congratulations on receiving the Silver Beaver Award for your long service in Scouting at the annual dinner of the Last Frontier Council Tuesday night.

The First Methodist Church and Scouting have worked together for more than forty years, and our program is largely due to the notable service of dedicated persons like yourself.

Through your many services for years you have helped build men—men of character—men who will continue to be loyal to all of the high values that have made America great.

All of us in the church are deeply indebted to you for your magnificent contributions to Scouting and to the church.

Sincerely yours,

Dear Mr. McKenzie:

Congratulations to you for starting the interdenominational religious services each Wednesday morning. I know that the request came from workers, but you are to be commended for giving this program such a high priority in your busy schedule.

Roy Winkle, one of your foremen who is a member of the Church of the Nazarene, told me how much the common bond established by prayer and song has reduced the number of grievances that normally arise among people working together. As Roy says, "These services have really boosted morale."

We as ministers realize that your Wednesday morning services have increased attendance at our churches and that folk who had long stayed away are now attending. We enjoy taking turns leading your services.

Your services are great and I hope that they will always be held.

Cordially yours,

Dear Mr. Mattox:

Congratulations to you and your committee of teachers and counselors for launching such a splendid program to reduce the number of high school dropouts.

I am alarmed when I read that more than one third of the nation's young people drop out of school before completing senior high school. And yet I am encouraged when I see the work of you and your committee in convincing the youth of Parksville that it pays to stay in school.

All of us in the community are grateful to you and your associates for the exceptional service which you are rendering.

Cordially yours,

Dear Mayor Stephenson:

As a citizen of Marshall I want to express my sincere appreciation of the many things you have done to make it a better place in which to live.

Your fine efforts to strengthen brotherhood in our city have done much to break down some of the barriers which exist.

You probably feel that yours has been a thankless task at times, but I can assure you that you have the gratitude of all of us in your courageous and positive leadership.

Cordially yours,

117

Dear Mr. Howery:

Congratulations! Never have I been so thrilled as I was to see "Price of Peace," the program which you directed at Municipal Auditorium Monday night.

In directing the massed choir from many churches and also in handling all of the details for such a production as this, you certainly revealed a masterful ability.

Speaking for the hundreds of persons who had the opportunity to see this moving pageant, I want to tell you how much we appreciate your outstanding work.

Sincerely yours,

Dear Mr. Malone:

Thank you so much for sending me a copy of the annual report of the Garden City Chamber of Commerce. It is complete and interesting and is an excellent portrayal of the many varied activities of the organization.

It is interesting to note the rapid growth in industrial enterprises, and I know that this is due largely to the zeal and planning of the expansion committee which guided the Chamber's Eastern tour.

All of us appreciate the tremendous amount of work and the many services which you render as secretary-manager of the Chamber of Commerce.

Cordially yours,

Dear Mr. Danielson:

In a day of competitive appeals there's nothing like the impact of the power of the press. For that reason I'm sure that your readers appreciate your Monday morning practice of running the highlights from a message given at a place of worship the day before under the title, "Sunday Sermon."

This is one of the most worthwhile services which "The Tulsa Tribune" renders to the people of our city, and I know that many of them would join me in expressing our deep appreciation to you for keeping a weekly focus on spiritual values.

Sincerely yours,

Dear Mr. Norfleet:

Not so many years ago when I moved to Jamestown so many people told me, "We have more than our share of commercialized amusements. Nothing cultural ever pays."

But after reading of the year's activities sponsored by the Community Series, I am convinced that our citizens now support many worthwhile programs.

You have done a marvelous job in bringing entertainment, culture, and enjoyment to many of us, and we are most grateful. We are most fortunate in having such excellent leadership for the coming year.

Sincerely yours,

Dear Mr. Berry:

I was very glad to learn that the Retail Merchants' Association will allow only floats with a religious theme in the Christmas parade this year.

Basically Christmas has the deepest religious significance, so we are happy to know that you and your committee will stress that fact in the parade.

Your announcement pleased all of us who serve as ministers, of course, but also hundreds of persons who are members of churches of our community.

Sincerely yours,

119

Dear Kenneth:

All of us at First Presbyterian Church wish to join with others in congratulating you upon the completion of your splendid new educational unit at your church.

After reading the many features of your new building in Sunday's "Phoenix" I am convinced that you have a structure which will meet the needs of your ever-growing congregation.

This fine accomplishment is a credit to your new unit, but in the meantime I wanted to send you best wishes from our congregation to you and your members.

Sincerely yours,

Dear Dr. Schilling:

In a day in which many values are being questioned, it is heartening to know that in your address at the district meeting of science teachers here Thursday you emphasized that the teaching of science should increase the awareness of God.

In reading excerpts from your address in the "Chicago Tribune" I was also interested in your statement, "Man's quest for understanding in science reinforces his quest for understanding in religion."

I'm very sure that all of us who believe in the worth of religious values appreciate your address to the science teachers.

Cordially yours,

Dear Mrs. Houser:

This is just a note in recognition of your splendid work as president of the Oak Park Women's Hospital Auxiliary for the past year.

You and your members—all 188 of them—deserve a world of credit for redecorating the chapel, setting up the snack bar, and adding books to the library. In your many activities you have rendered an outstanding service to all who use the hospital facilities.

All of us at First Methodist Church thank you for your fine contribution to the life of this community and congratulate you upon your excellent work.

Cordially yours,

Dear Kenneth:

Heartiest congratulations on winning first place for your X-ray project at the tenth annual Joplin Public School Science Fair.

This is a noteworthy achievement, indeed, when your exhibit placed first in the final exhibits from four high schools and six junior high schools.

I know the hours of work required in your project which covered studies important in the manufacture of transistors, crystal oscillators, and other electronic instruments.

We rejoice with you in your success!

Sincerely yours,

Hearty congratulations,
Larry,

. . . on starting the meditation period at Bristol High School at 7:45 each morning. It's good news to hear that this program which you sparked as president of the Student Council is growing in interest and attendance.

You and your friends know what Paul Dietzel, football coach at West Point, meant when he said recently, "When the day of a game comes, I begin it as I begin every day: with a recommitment of my life to God."

121

My sincere best wishes to all of you who realize that commitment to religious values gives life direction and power.

Cordially yours,

Dear Jay,

It's a marvelous service which you and your fellow amateur radio operators over the nation perform in serving as a network for the eighty eye banks through the country.

I was amazed to learn how you and your friends relay information through the "Eye Bank Network" on the need for transplants and the availability of eyes.

Permit me to express my great admiration to you and your friends in using your hobby to help restore sight to the blind.

Sincerely yours,

Dear Jean:

Heartiest congratulations upon your election as vice-president of the Religious Newswriters Association for the coming year.

Your excellent coverage of religious activities and trends in Dayton is greatly appreciated not only by church leaders but also by the thousands of church members.

Keep up the good work!

Sincerely yours,

WELCOME TO A NEW MINISTER

Dear Dr. Huntington:

Welcome to Warrensburg!

When I read in Tuesday's "Globe" that you were leaving your post in Columbia to become minister of the Crown Heights Baptist Church here, I was delighted.

122

Delighted—yes, for two reasons. First, I have enjoyed your radio series, "Confident Living," for several years, and I have often wished that you were closer to Warrensburg so that we might get together. Second, we are all glad that you are coming because Crown Heights has a wonderful membership, and I know that your ministry here will be a glorious one.

In the meantime please let me know if there is anything that I can do for you before your arrival.

Sincerely yours,

UPON ACCOMPLISHMENT OF SON

Dear Jim and Gertrude:

I read in last night's "Times" that your son, Edward, had been chosen for membership in Blue Key, leadership fraternity at the University of Kentucky. Of all the honors that have come to him, I believe this is one of the most outstanding.

You have every reason to be proud of Edward and his fine record. Mrs. Woodrum joins me in this word of congratulations.

Cordially yours,

UPON RETIREMENT OF A SCHOOL TEACHER

Dear Mrs. Cromer:

There are some letters that it is a joy to write and this is one of them.

Forty-two years of dedicated teaching—enriching the lives of thousands of youngsters—is a record of service which few persons achieve. It is also a record which deserves a sincere word of gratitude from all of those whom you have helped so generously during these years.

As you retire from active teaching, I want to add my congratulations to you for your splendid record of service.

123

Teaching isn't easy. I taught for two years. You and I appreciate the lighthearted interpretation of the teacher as voiced by an unknown writer: "A teacher is courage with Kleenex in her pocket, sympathy with a snowsuit, and patience with papers to grade. She stands tall before sniffles, squirmings, stomach aches, spills, sloth, or sauciness. Neither does she disintegrate before tears, trifles, excuses; parents who spout, boys who shout, or girls who pout. She is somebody who likes somebody else's children and still has strength enough left to go to a PTA meeting."

No words of mine can do justice to your record of service, but I'm sure that many have found inspiration in your leadership and that many more will find a worthy example in your fine record.

Cordially yours,

UPON RETIREMENT FROM BUSINESS

Dear Mr. Wantland:

Word of your retirement from business, which reached me today, occasions this letter of congratulations and best wishes.

You have contributed greatly to the progress of the dry cleaning business in serving as an officer of the Missouri Drycleaners' Association. I am sure no man has ever left behind him a finer record of loyalty and devotion to the highest type of business ideals.

Knowing your love for fishing, and with ample time now yours, I wish you the best of luck in catching the biggest one ever!

Sincerely yours,

UPON OBSERVANCE OF NATIONAL WEEK

Dear Mrs. Capper:

The celebration of National Business and Professional Women's Week offers, because of the magnificent work done by women in business and the professions, an excellent opportunity for us to pay tribute to all members of this splendid group.

No nation is greater than its women. We need the leadership, the special skills in human relationships, and the vision and devotion of women in the affairs of the community, state, and nation.

So I'd like to extend to you and your members our hearty thanks and appreciation for your many notable contributions to community life—contributions which add to the security, health, comfort, and happiness of us all.

Sincerely yours,

UPON ANNIVERSARY OF BUSINESS

Dear Mr. Page:

On the eve of your Thirtieth Business Anniversary I want to extend to you my congratulations on your record of achievement and my sincere best wishes for the future.

Through the years you and your associates and employees have sponsored so many worthwhile activities for community betterment.

You have won the respect and confidence of our people, and you have every right to be proud of the excellent reputation of your store.

Sincerely yours,

UPON CELEBRATION OF A BIRTHDAY

Dear Mr. Newcomb:

Today I was very pleased to hear that you will observe your birthday next Saturday, and I want to send you this brief message of congratulations and my sincere wish that you will enjoy the best of health for years to come.

In serving so many years as chairman of the 89'ers Commission, you have rendered a service so splendid that all Oklahomans are indebted to you.

I hope that your birthday will be a happy occasion, and since service to others is the real measure of happiness, I know it will be.

Sincerely yours,

UPON PROMOTION

Dear Cal:

John O'Neil told me this morning that you will soon be leaving your present position to become director of public relations for the Barrett Manufacturing Company.

I wanted to send you this word of congratulations and best wishes, for I am happy to learn of your advancement to a position of greater responsibility and opportunity.

You've rendered a lot of service civic-wise and we shall miss you.

The best of luck to you in your new work!

Cordially yours,

Congratulations,
Chief Finnerty,

. . . upon your promotion to chief of the Lewisburg Fire Department! Your selection for this position of greater responsibility is a high compliment to your character and integrity.

You'll serve most ably in this position, and I know that I voice the thoughts of all citizens in wishing you the best in your new post.

Sincerely yours,

COURTESY NOTE TO YOUTH LEADER

Dear Mr. Cordell:

It was a real pleasure to see you again and to meet with your fine group of young people when you made a special tour of our new church Wednesday afternoon.

How fine it is that you are giving so much time to youth and helping them to know more about the character-building agencies in our community.

Please let me know if I can ever be of help to you in your splendid program.

Cordially yours,

Let's face it: The demands on your time to promote the welfare of individuals and groups—inside and outside your congregation—will increase. But take the time to write more friendly letters to "key" individuals of your city. This extra effort will strengthen the impact of your church on those who "cross the crowded ways of life." Join with others who are improving the spiritual climate of your community and thus cement harmonious relationships by writing more good-will letters.

127

14

WINNING
good will in the parish

Have you ever asked yourself, "Am I losing touch with my congregation"? It's a searching question, a natural question. Burdened and working overtime, you can never make as many personal contacts as you'd like.

But the fact remains: How successful, efficient, and influential you are as a minister depends to a great degree on staying in touch with as many of your members as possible. Every day you face the challenge of keeping your congregation (as individuals) interested and also growing in spiritual maturity. Above all, you seek nothing save the privilege of lifting and enriching the lives of your members, bringing them into true Christian fellowship.

What's more, you know that to knit together the fellowship of your church membership means more than worshiping together. And this doesn't mean that you step up the number of social affairs. "The Christian community must be a community of friends," says George Barnes Edgar, pastor of the First Presbyterian Church, Fort Pierce, Florida, "so we try to make opportunity in the life of the church for the development of friendship. But we believe that above all else, the church is the body of Christ."

Just as the rest of the world has changed, so has the life of the minister been altered. Unlike the clergyman of yesterday —who led a rather quiet, contemplative life—today's minister must spend so much time in church administration that he cannot spend as must time counseling the wistful, worried, and bereaved people as he would like.

Your grandfather's preacher was deeply involved in the lives of all who made up his small flock. As a result he shared the joys and sorrows—practically all experiences—which came to members of his congregation.

But that has all changed. Today's pastor must direct a maze of activities, groups, committees, and know as many members as possible as individuals. Pastors of metropolitan churches now spend half their time in various types of administration, Gibson Winter reveals in his book, *The Suburban Captivity of the Churches.*

Vital spiritual tasks—calling on the sick, various members, and prospective members; counseling; tending to weddings and funerals; preparation of sermons—all these are typical demands made by the responsibilities of your calling. And you may feel like one busy minister who confessed, "Every time I ring a doorbell my conscience asks, 'Is this where I am needed most?' "

With such a tremendous increase in the number of activities the minister has an extremely difficult time trying to cope with the demands of his time and energy. H. Richard Niebuhr and others in their book, *The Purpose of the Church and Its Ministry,* describe the contemporary minister as a "pastoral director," and suggest that the new minister may emerge as a "democratic pastoral administrator, that is to say, one responsible for holding in balance, invigorating, and maintaining communication among a host of activities and their responsible leaders, all directed toward a common end."

Are you "maintaining communication"? Are you staying in touch with many members of the church family—officers, those performing special duties, members—all who are co-workers with you in building the Kingdom? Not as much as you would like? Then strengthen your ministry by writing more good-will letters.

Personal letters are best, of course, because they reach out through space and cement members' loyalty and build support. But you may also use well-written form letters done in a personalized fashion. In fact, you should use both kinds in strengthening the ties of church loyalty. As a result you will extend the power of your ministry in countless lives.

Just how do you decide when to write one? That's easy. Keep your imagination alive, and you will see that types of good-will letters which may be utilized are practically limitless. The point is: Don't be content to write the usual letters for the usual situations. You will see new opportunities constantly as you live a part of your life in the lives of your members.

Note how the following specimens show innumerable ways of using personal and form letters in building devotion, co-operation, enthusiasm, friendship, appreciation, and loyalty.

ACKNOWLEDGMENT OF APPRECIATION

Dear Tom:

Like yourself, I have always believed that everything we have is in sacred trust and that we are stewards of all that we are and all that we possess.

You have certainly shown yourself a devoted steward in making the beautiful cabinets for the children's division. Your idea of using shelves and storage space will make it easy for teachers to keep everything in one central location.

In behalf of the Board of Education, the teachers, and the children, I would like to express our sincere thanks to you.

Your generous and constant help is deeply appreciated.

Sincerely yours,

Dear Fred:

"I love thy church, O God."

Those words to the old hymn have a new meaning for me and to members of our congregation. And it's all because of something glorious which you did.

When you were presented with a check for $2,000 (for the hundreds of hours which you spent in drawing plans, talking to contractors, getting bids on air-conditioning equipment and performing so many other professional tasks) at the last board meeting and then you declined and asked that it be given to the church treasurer to be used as needed, we saw a great act of Christian belief and dedication.

Your glorious example will make all of us aware that only as we share do we grow richer spiritually. Truly your act will bring new meaning and dedication to all of us who can show that we love God's church.

Cordially yours,

Dear Mrs. Matlock:

Progress is measured by people—people who give of their best through the years. Without the loyalty and devotion of dedicated persons like yourself our church would have never grown in spiritual power.

That's why it's such a pleasure to write you this note of thanks for serving as a Sunday school teacher for ten years. You have touched the lives of many children, and I know that they appreciate your counsel and inspiration.

All of us on the church staff are grateful to you for your sacrificial service, and we pray that God may continue to bless you in your wonderful work.

Sincerely yours,

Dear Bruce:

You've probably noticed that the world is full of willing people. Some willing to work and others willing to let them.

You certainly proved worthy of the first category when you rushed to the church at 5 a.m. last Sunday when the heating unit went on the blink. Gomer Bittle, our custodian, told of calling you and how with your engineering know-how you soon had everything functioning fine about thirty minutes later.

All members of the First Presbyterian Church would join me in thanking you for your service.

Sincerely yours,

Dear Haskell:

Your creative spark is just the thing we need to make Loyalty Sunday a great success!

Last night I read the series of compelling promotional letters which you prepared for this occasion. Your letters have zest, appeal, inspiration, excellent continuity—all the qualities that should make them the most effective ones we've ever used.

Congratulations and thanks for a job well done!

Cordially yours,

Dear Mr. Bryant:

In a day in which many moral values are toppling, you deserve our thanks for presenting the two films, "Page of Death" and "Perversion for Profit," at the recent district rally for young people of our churches.

Both the films carry strong impact, and I know that all of the youngsters who saw them will recognize the dangers of obscene literature.

132

Feel free to use my name as a reference, if you wish, in booking these films in other cities of the state. And thank you so much for presenting them to our group.

Cordially yours,

Dear Mrs. Strickler:

How can we thank you for serving as a teacher in our primary department for eight years?

Maybe Janet, my daughter, expressed it best when she came home Sunday and said, "If God had enough helpers like Mrs. Strickler, he wouldn't have to work so hard."

All of us on the church staff were genuinely sorry to hear of your resignation. But we are so grateful to you for your years of dedicated service—a service which will continue as all the children whom you have taught lead lives of Christian usefulness and honor.

"Well done!"

Gratefully yours,

Dear Roland:

"Just what we've been looking for!"

That was the unanimous reaction of members of the missions committee when I explained your idea of setting up a "scholarship plate banquet" to help support students who are preparing for full-time Christian service.

Members of the group are now discussing publicity plans, possible dates, what might be charged for the plates, and other details. You will be invited to attend the next meeting.

All of us here at First Community Church—and many youths in the future who will train for the ministry and other areas—would join me in saying "Thank you!"

Cordially yours,

133

Dear Mrs. Danner:

You're a good-will ambasssador for the North Broadway Christian Church in fulfilling your duties as a member of the every-member-visitation group.

What you say about the church—its policies, its services, personnel, history, problems—is vitally important.

That's why I hope you'll enjoy the enclosed pamphlet, "How It Happened." You'll find many interesting facts about the church—facts you may not have known.

And after you've read it, you'll be better informed for your role as a good-will ambassador!

Sincerely yours,

Dear Mrs. Mixon:

How proud you must be of Dick for being awarded the huge Christmas candle, symbolic of outstanding service to the church, at the dinner Wednesday night.

And you have a right to be. Fourteen years of dedicated service as a teacher with the class tripled in size are really achievements of note. I am mighty proud of him, too.

One of the biggest reasons for his wonderful work is the cooperation and encouragement which he gets from you. His work is more than a Sunday job. In sponsoring outings, craft classes, a basketball team, and other activities, he frequently works with the boys at nights and on weekends.

So let me say again how grateful I am to Dick for his service to boyhood and church, but I am also very grateful to you for your help and understanding.

Cordially yours,

Dear Mrs. Goggans:

Yesterday afternoon I was talking to Mrs. James Holland and she said, "You will never know how much we appreciate the marvelous help which Mrs. Goggans always gives to every new teacher."

Her high praise for you reminded me that many other teachers through the years have told me how much you have helped them, not just in their first Sundays but on other occasions.

You possess an unusual gift, Mrs. Goggans, in that you give each new teacher a sense of belonging, of doing a great job in building the Kingdom. What's more, you inspire each person to do his best.

Your excellent work as superintendent of the children's division is deeply appreciated. We have a loyal and competent group of teachers largely because of your leadership and inspiration.

Sincerely yours,

Dear Truman:

"Very striking!"

That's the comment of all to whom I've shown your photograph of the Bates family which we plan to use in our back-to-church campaign next month.

Your excellent photograph ties in admirably with our theme —"Show Them the Way—This Week."

Members of the promotion committee join me in thanking you for taking this excellent photograph.

Cordially yours,

ACKNOWLEDGMENT OF CONGRATULATIONS

Dear Albert:

Thank you for your cheering words regarding the album, "Music from the Heart of the City," which was recorded by our chancel choir as a part of the seventy-fifth anniversary of the First Methodist Church in Oklahoma City.

135

As one of the seven original churches here we thought that the album could memorialize the founding of the church a few days following the Run of 1889.

As you know, proceeds from the sale of the albums will go toward a fund to buy new robes for the chancel choir. I'll appreciate your permitting us to use excerpts from your letter among the "testimonials" in a promotion piece to be sent to members of the congregation.

Sincerely yours,

ACKNOWLEDGMENT OF THANK-YOU NOTE

Dear Mrs. Frye:

Thank you, sincerely, for your nice note. We are all happy to know that you and members of your club enjoyed the banquet in Rinehart Hall at the church December 12.

I have sent your letter to Mrs. Eva Dunagan, who has charge of the kitchen, and also to Charles Lesly, the custodian who helped in so many ways. They will appreciate your thoughtfulness in writing.

Thank you again for your thoughtful letter.

Cordially yours,

ACKNOWLEDGMENT OF RESIGNATION FROM POSITION

Dear Wendell:

I regretted, indeed, receiving your letter of resignation from the board of trustees.

Of course, I realize that your decision was reached because your new position at Sloan Bros. will require more time as you visit dealers and distributors over a large territory.

136

All of us who have worked with you will miss your sound counsel and your genial presence at board meetings. You were especially helpful in helping us to solve so many problems when the sanctuary was remodeled two years ago.

I know that others share with me a deep sense of gratitude for all you have contributed to the progress of Riverside Presbyterian Church.

Cordially yours,

CONGRATULATIONS FOR WINNING

Dear Jerry:

Heartiest congratulations to you and members of your team in winning second in the all-city softball league! All of us at St. John's are proud of you.

By winning two straight—7 to 4 from the Lutherans, and 4 to 2 from the Oakwood Baptists, in the quarter finals and the semi-finals—you and your hustling players demonstrated unusual skill and stamina.

Without your interest and fine coaching I am certain that our club would not have placed so high. When I heard the results on my return from Denver, I immediately realized what a remarkable job you had done in view of the heavy loss of talent from last year's team.

Best wishes for a winning team next year!

Sincerely yours,

Dear Clifford:

How does it feel to be a celebrity?

After all, few churches can boast of a golf champion within their ranks. Isn't it natural that we're all much impressed and fairly bursting with pride?

137

Heartiest congratulations on winning the state amateur title at the Twin Oaks Country Club, and may you wear the crown for many years to come!

Cordially yours,

ACKNOWLEDGMENT OF VALUABLE SUGGESTION

Dear Andrew:

I am very enthusiastic about your proposal for a public relations manual for our church. Such a publication is needed, and I appreciate your showing me a tentative table of contents.

If convenient I shall appreciate your meeting with Leonard Harrison, Jimmy Hoyler, and myself in my office Tuesday afternoon at 3:30. At that time we can make plans for writing the copy and decide what format to use.

Thank you for your excellent idea and for your offer to gather and write material for several sections.

Sincerely yours,

Dear Victor:

Kenneth May told me today that you are the person responsible for setting up a "hospitality desk" at the entrance of the Education Building.

This is just a word to thank you for making a real contribution to our Sunday school program. Committee members can now do a better job in greeting members and guests and can direct newcomers to the proper classes.

Cordially yours,

REGRET OF MOVE TO ANOTHER CITY

Dear Mr. and Mrs. Haddican:

This is just a brief little note to express our best wishes to you as you move to Williamstown.

138

Both of you have contributed so much not only to the First Christian Church but to community groups here in Durant. Your wonderful help in working with the youth groups, especially at summer camps, makes us all indebted to both of you.

You will find Williamstown an excellent community, and I have already written Roger Hubbard, pastor of the Park Hill Christian Church, about your coming.

Our sincere best wishes and our prayers go with you.

Cordially yours,

ARRANGEMENT OF A SOCIAL EVENT

Dear Mrs. Davenport:

You are certainly to be congratulated for arranging such a fine party for Mrs. Morren at the church Tuesday night.

All of the well-wishers who attended the party and the reception are most grateful to you. And the caricatures that you created to show some of the milestones in Mrs. Morren's life added so much to the occasion.

Congratulations on a job well done!

Sincerely yours,

REQUEST FOR RETURN OF BOOK

Dear Mr. Barbour:

Don't apologize.

I send out reminders from time to time. Yes, and I receive them, too.

I haven't the slightest worry about your willingness to return "Characteristics of Jesus" by W. McFerrin Stowe which you checked out of the church library several months ago. Two new

139

staff members would like to use it in a special study series that they are planning.

Drop it by the church or send it by mail. We'll surely appreciate it.

Sincerely yours,

INVITATION TO SERVE

Dear Wayne:

Sharing!

This is the one universal language of Christian love that millions of Americans will have an opportunity to demonstrate in the One Great Hour of Sharing in which our church will participate with others on Sunday, March 8.

As you probably know, in this observance it is possible for Church World Service, through contributions to local churches throughout the nation to respond to the destitute and disaster-stricken overseas.

Did you know, for example, that $10 will give bread to 9,000 needy persons? Or that $5 will give a slice of bread and a cup of milk daily to 350 refugee children for 10 weeks?

Because of your intense interest in world service and your talent for getting things done, I would like so much for you to direct the observance in our church. Enclosed are some news stories, promotion helps, and other material. Let me know how I can help in this program to reach the needy of the world.

Sincerely yours,

Dear Mrs. Dobry:

Our church needs your help! When I feel that something is of great importance, I always turn to people like you for assistance, because I know how loyal you are to Travis Park Methodist Church.

Our second Neighborhood Group Meeting is scheduled for Monday, March 26, at 7:30 p.m. I would like for you to be the leader of one of these groups. Your presentation will be simple but of the greatest importance. I shall personally meet with you and ninety-nine others on Sunday, March 25, at 9:30 a.m. in Stewardship Hall for instruction and assignments.

I am sure that you will help us; therefore, it is imperative that you be present on Sunday, March 25, at 9:30 a.m. in Stewardship Hall for the period of instruction. I know you will do all in your power to render this important service.

Please use the enclosed card to let me know whether or not you can assist us.

Sincerely yours,[1]

CONGRATULATIONS TO COLLEGE GRADUATE

Dear Jane:

My hearty congratulations upon your graduation from the University of New Mexico! This is a significant occasion in your life, and all of us at Hollywood-Beverly Church are justly proud of you!

No doubt the reality of Christianity has become very evident to you, and I am sure the church will continue to influence your future.

I hope that you will always count me your friend, as well as your minister. I am very much interested in your future and covet any opportunity to help you. May God bless you always!

Faithfully yours, [2]

[1] Used by J. Walter Browers, minister, Travis Park Methodist Church, San Antonio, Tex.
[2] Used by Myron C. Cole, minister, Hollywood-Beverly Christian Church, Hollywood, Calif.

Dear Dave:

As your home church minister let me join your relatives and friends in extending congratulations upon your graduation. An ancient Roman author said, "Endurance is the final test of mortals." You have met that test successfully. I know that your education will continue whether in the academic sense or not. You have my heartiest good wishes for continued progress.

May you find many durable satisfactions in life.

Sincerely yours, [3]

Dear Mrs. Hubble:

I was told today that you have completed all requirements for your Master of Arts degree at University of Kansas City and that you will receive the degree this week.

You deserve a lot of credit for this achievement, because I know you have attended night classes for two years in addition to working full time plus serving as an officer in the Wesleyan Service Guild.

You have shown a lot of spirit and determination, and I know that I speak for your many friends in sending you heartiest congratulations for your newest accomplishment.

Cordially yours,

THANK-YOU FOR ALTAR FLOWERS

Dear Mrs. Strandberg:

Just a note to tell you that the memorial poinsettia, which you gave to the church last Sunday, not only brought added beauty to both of the morning church services, but it also carried some of the spirit of Christmas to another group.

[3] Used by David A. MacLennan, minister, Brick Presbyterian Church, Rochester, N.Y.

Members of the visitation committee of the Guild took all the plants to nursing homes Sunday afternoon. Your plant was taken to Littlefield Manor where it brings beauty to all of the elderly men and women who live there.

Sincerely yours,

Dear Mrs. Westbrook:

I want to extend this personal word of appreciation to you for the beautiful altar flowers which you so graciously placed in our sanctuary Sunday. What a lovely way to remember your beloved husband and pay tribute to him in honor of his birthday.

With kindest good wishes and appreciation.

Sincerely yours,[4]

INVITATION TO CHOIR REUNION

To All Former Christ
Church Choir Members

Sunday, January 6, is the date of the Annual Choir Reunion. The service will be held at 4:00 p.m. in the church, at which time Christ Church Choir will present its annual service of Christmas Music.

Former choir members are asked to meet in the Parish Hall at 3:40 p.m. to receive music and hymnals, preparatory to taking part in the processional through the church. This service is something to which we all look forward with a great deal of pleasure. Let us make this the finest choir reunion we have ever had.

[4] Used by Kenneth A. Carlson, minister, First Methodist Church, Glendale, Calif.

143

A Coffee Hour for former choir members and their families will be held in the Parish Hall following the service.

Sincerely yours,[5]

CONGRATULATIONS ON ELECTION

Dear Fellow Officer:

We congratulate you upon your election to one of the official boards of First Presbyterian Church. This choice involves both an honor to you and a responsibility of Christian leadership in the congregation. We look forward to serving with you in advancing the cause of Jesus Christ in this place and to the ends of the earth.

The ordination and installation of all newly elected officers will take place in connection with the 11:00 service on Sunday, January 1. I am enclosing a mimeographed sheet indicating the procedure for these services.

All officers of the three boards will meet at 10:45 that morning with the deacons in the Chapel, elders in the parlor, and the trustees in the library. They will then proceed down the aisle following the choir, with the elders and trustees in the south line and the deacons in the north line. At the proper time in the service we will proceed as indicated on the enclosed sheet.

It is imperative that all of us be present. If for some good reason it is absolutely impossible for you to be there, please notify my office so that we can make some other arrangement for your ordination and installation.

Yours sincerely,[6]

[5] Used by Charles E. Sutton, rector, Christ Episcopal Church, Reading, Pa. From "Church Choir Reunions," by A. Stanley Keast, *Church Business*, December, 1957, and reprinted by special permission from the Duplex Envelope Company, Richmond, Va.

[6] Used by C. Ralston Smith, minister, First Presbyterian Church, Oklahoma City, Okla.

THANK-YOU TO A RETIRING DEACON

Dear Bill:

I feel a sense of personal loss in contemplating the fact that you have shared your last meeting as an active member of the deacons. You have been loyal, helpful, and graciously co-operative through the years you have served as deacon.

Of course, I know your interest in the church will continue. I will feel free to call on you for tasks that need you, and I know you will respond as you always have in the past.

Believe me when I say I am deeply grateful for your friend-ship, your generous service to the church, and your encourage-ment to the ministers and the staff. Thank you sincerely.

May God bless and guide you and yours through the years to come.

Affectionately,[7]

THANK-YOU TO A RETIRING TRUSTEE

Dear Charlie:

To the words expressed to you and the others retiring from the board this month at the December 4 Board of Trustees meet-ing, I wish to add a personal word.

Your membership on this important board of our church has meant much to the church here, and at large. To conduct the "temporal affairs" of Christ's church as the board has done proves that the division between "things temporal" and "spiri-tual" is an artificial one.

I have been greatly heartened in my ministry at Brick to have you share in it at the executive level.

You have earned the "sabbatical leave" of one year which the Constitution provides; however, I know that you will retain

[7] Used by Harold B. Walker, minister, First Presbyterian Church, Evanston, Ill.

145

your interest and that we may turn to you for leadership again in the near future.

My best thanks to you for all you have meant to the church through the last three years as a trustee.

God bless you and yours always.

Sincerely,[8]

CONGRATULATIONS ON GOLDEN WEDDING ANNIVERSARY

Dear Mr. and Mrs. McChesney:

I want to join with your many friends in extending these words of congratulations on the occasion of your Golden Wedding Anniversary. What a wonderful privilege it is to have shared so many years of your life together, and certainly you have a great treasure of memories with which to live. Mrs. Carlson joins me in extending our every good wish for your continued happiness.

It is a real privilege for me to be minister of the church with which you have been affiliated for so many years. If I can be of service to you at any time, please do not hesitate to call upon me.

Cordially, and with kindest personal regards,[9]

LETTER TO FIFTY-YEAR MEMBER

Dear Mr. Preston:

The enclosed Fifty-Year Certificate of Membership is sent to you with our heartiest felicitations. It is really an achievement to be a member of the church for half a century.

[8] Used by David A. MacLennan, minister, Brick Presbyterian Church, Rochester, N.Y.
[9] Used by Kenneth A. Carlson, minister, First Methodist Church, Glendale, Calif.

We were sorry that we could not present the certificate to you in person at our Annual Meeting on January 24, but we understand how difficult it would have been for you to come.

We are proud of you and your fellow members who united with our church fifty years ago. May God who has guided and guarded you this far continue to be your companion and strength in the years to come.

With warmest personal greetings.

Your friend and minister,[10]

EXPRESSION OF CONDOLENCE AND SYMPATHY

Dear Gerald:

I did not know about your father's sudden passing until I received a note from Morton Scott this morning. I am deeply sorry to learn of it.

To me your father personified all of the high ideals which make men great. In working with him at St. Stephens I soon discovered that he was a man of God in every way—in business, in sports, in civic work, in everything. He was admired and respected by all who knew him.

Never have I known anyone with a higher sense of the values which really make life worthwhile. It is my prayer that you and your mother will look to him who can show us "the way, the truth and the life."

Cordially yours,

Dear Mrs. Greenway:

I was shocked to hear on the TV newscast this morning of the passing of your husband, whose friendship it has been my privilege to enjoy for so many years.

[10] Used by David A. MacLennan, minister, Brick Presbyterian Church, Rochester, N.Y.

George Greenway will be missed by all who knew him. Few men have ever possessed so large a capacity for friendship. At all times he shared his best with others, and he was happiest when doing something for others.

I extend my sincere sympathy to you in your bereavement. But I know you will gain a certain measure of strength from the knowledge that your husband will live in honor in the memory of all who share your loss.

Sincerely yours,

Dear Albert:

I wish there were a way by which a friend could actually take over part of the sorrow of another friend and share it with him. How I would like to share yours. You do have my heartfelt sympathy in this time of sorrow in the death of your brother.

In him I am,

Faithfully yours,[11]

Dear Mrs. Bardock:

I am so very sorry to learn of the passing of your beloved sister. Words are always so inadequate in such moments to express the deeper feelings of the heart, but I am sure that it has been a source of strength for you to know that the prayers of your many friends have been undergirding you through these many hours.

It is good to know that the Reverend Mr. Root was privileged to share with you in the memorial service. I am sure that you found his ministry, on behalf of all of us, to be helpful, comforting, and inspirational.

[11] Used by W. R. Pettigrew, minister, Walnut Street Baptist Church, Louisville, Ky.

Mrs. Carlson joins me in this expression of our deepest sympathy. Blessings on you through the tomorrows and be sure of our continued concern and prayers.

Cordially,[12]

LETTER TO THE BEREAVED AT CHRISTMAS

Dear Mrs. Ferber:

I want you to know how much you are in my thoughts these days at Christmastide. Since the last observance of the birthday of Christ, you have lost a dear one. I know it has been difficult for you to make the adjustment.

"Time brings roses," declares an ancient proverb. They cannot be grown overnight. To the Christian the bud appears and then finally the rose in full bloom. Comfort in sorrow is like a rose—it does not come quickly. The wound heals only gradually, but it does heal, for God never fails us. He sends Time to be our healing minister.

I could not help sending this thought to you at the season of the year when I am sure your heart is a bit heavy. The significance of Christmas reminds us of the Christian's hopes. It gives us renewed faith and a realization that God does care.

Very sincerely yours,[13]

CHRISTMAS GREETING TO RADIO CONGREGATION

Dear Radio Friends:

You have been so friendly and helpful to me during these months of adjustment. Your letters have given me real strength.

[12] Used by Kenneth A. Carlson, minister, First Methodist Church, Glendale, Calif.

[13] Used by Myron C. Cole, pastor, Hollywood-Beverly Christian Church, Hollywood, Calif.

I know that I have been undergirded by your prayers—I can feel the Lord's presence.

In this Advent season I want to send you a special greeting to let you know that I keep you in my prayers.

Mrs. Uphoff joins me in wishing you a very Blessed Christmas and a Happy New Year.

> "Love came down at Christmas,
> Love all lovely, Love Divine;
> Love was born at Christmas
> Star and angels gave the sign.
>
> . . . .
>
> Love shall be our token,
> Love be yours and love be mine,
> Love to God and all men,
> Love for plea and gift and sign."

Sincerely yours,[14]

ANNOUNCEMENT,
CONGREGATIONAL MEMORIAL SERVICE

Dear Mr. Page:

Each year on the last Sunday of the year, First Methodist Church provides a congregational Memorial Service in the sanctuary to pay tribute to the members of our church who during the year have entered the Church Triumphant.

This year we will hold the service at 9:00 a.m. on Sunday, December 29. This letter comes as a special invitation to you and others in your family to attend this service, since included in those being memorialized will be your wife, Mrs. Henry F. Page.

The service is one of affirmative Christian faith and is not calculated to duplicate the services held at the time of your

[14] Used by Robert A. Uphoff, minister, First Methodist Church, Seattle, Wash.

loved one's death. It is an opportunity for us as a congregation to remember these our members and friends in a service of worship which will call to our attention the resources of our religious faith.

As a symbol of remembrance the altar vases will be filled with roses that morning. One of the roses will be in memory of your wife. The roses will remain on the altar during the second service (though the Memorial Service will be conducted only at 9 o'clock), and then we would be happy for you to have the rose. You may pick it up at the church office or make arrangements with Mrs. Green for securing it after the second service.

My sermon will be on the theme "One World Is Not Enough" and will be an effort to point up for all of us the basic Christian faith in life eternal.

Sincerely yours,[15]

COUNSEL IN A DIVORCE SITUATION

Dear Sandra:

I regret that you are having such a difficult time, but I am afraid that this has to be expected with anyone who has gone through what you have these past months. This does not make it any easier for you, I know, especially when you are so far away from family and friends.

To fail, and be forced to admit to oneself and the world this failure, is difficult indeed. But I know that you have the courage and the conviction that you did the very best that you could under the circumstances. It is human to have moments of regret, of self-flagellation, even self-pity, but try not to give in to these times. It is normal to think about the past—situations come up daily which remind us of things which have happened before. But try to remember the best parts of your marriage and use

[15] Used by Hoover Rupert, minister, First Methodist Church, Ann Arbor, Mich.

them constructively in preparing for the future. Your attitudes toward yourself and toward Roy now may make the difference in your adjustment to a possible future marriage.

The time now and in the days ahead can be a time of growth and development in self-understanding. Try to make each day count by trying something new or making new friends. Your new situation can change old relationships and lead to new ones. Make an effort to think of yourself as an individual and not as a part of someone else. This can be a learning time, a time of making your own decisions, of discovering yourself as a person. This period in your life is a second chance—a chance to correct mistakes made in the past and go on to a new beginning. Too few have this opportunity—many would give a great deal to have it. I know that with daily prayer for God's help and guidance, you will have the strength and courage to make the most of this gift.

My thoughts and prayers are with you always and especially at this Eastertime. Please write whenever you feel the need and know of my desire to be of help whenever and wherever I can. God bless you.

Sincerely yours,[16]

PRAYERS FOR MEMBERS DURING LENT

Dear Friend:

On Wednesday mornings during Lent, I plan to be at the altar of First Methodist Church in prayer for our church and for each of its members, praying for a different group of persons by name each week.

On next Wednesday morning, I plan to remember you and your family in prayer before the altar at 9:00 a.m. If it would be convenient for you to be present at the church at that time to join your prayers with mine, I cordially invite you to do so.

[16] Used by Lance Webb, while serving as minister, North Broadway Methodist Church, Columbus, Ohio.

If you have any special needs for which you would wish prayers, I would appreciate knowing of them. If you would like to speak to me about any need, I would be happy to have the opportunity to speak with you and to pray with you immediately after the brief prayer service which should last from 9:00 to 9:30 a.m.

I am convinced that our God is able to hear and answer prayers, and that new life will come to our church only as we become more concerned about and pray for one another.

I hope to see you at the altar in prayer with me next Wednesday at 9:00 a.m., if this is at all convenient for you. If you cannot be present, please remember me and your church in your prayers wherever you may be at that hour.

Sincerely, your pastor,[17]

BIRTHDAY LETTER TO PRESCHOOL CHILD

Dear Susan:

You are having a birthday! I am so glad.

This is to tell you so, and to say that I will be saying "thank you" to our Heavenly Father for sending you to your family and to us here in Brick Church.

May you have a lovely birthday and another year of health and joy, and growth, too.

Here is a prayer Mother or Daddy could help you say on your birthday:

> "Heavenly Father, hear my prayer,
> Keep us in Thy loving care.
> Guard us through the livelong day,
> In our work and in our play.

[17] Used by Donald B. Strobe, minister, First Methodist Church, Eaton Rapids, Mich.

> Keep us pure and sweet and true
> In everything we say and do. Amen."

May the dear Lord bless you. I send you my love.

Your friend at the church,[18]

PASTORAL LETTER FOR NEW CHURCH YEAR

Dear Friends:

I am writing this, my seventeenth pastoral letter, in a log cabin among the Vermont hills. The window of the little room that serves me as a study commands a breathtaking view of Mount Mansfield. There is no other dwelling in sight, and for one whose work is done in New York with its crowds and clatter the solitude and silence are a boon.

Yet it was with something akin to reluctance that I left New York at the end of July to come to this hideaway. So much was happening in the city and the nation, particularly on the civil rights front, to make one want to be close to the developing situation. The United States has a social revolution on its hands, and the Christian church is caught up in it, its role not that of spectator but participant.

Gone are the days when Christians could be content to construe their churchmanship solely in terms of personal piety —attendance at church on Sundays, saying their prayers, reading the Bible. Personal piety that lacks social concern is rightly suspect; it can be the worst kind of selfishness. The churches have been insisting for long enough, mostly by means of resolutions and manifestos, that Christianity is concerned with the whole of life and not merely the segment of it marked off as religious. The time has come to back up words with deeds.

As Christians we have been altogether too withdrawn from the world, our religion in the main a Sunday activity, our influ-

[18] Used by David A. MacLennan, minister, Brick Presbyterian Church, Rochester, N.Y.

154

ence and impact on national life peripheral. Whitehead, pointing this out, could say of Protestantism: "Its dogmas no longer dominate; its divisions no longer interest; its institutions no longer direct the patterns of life." The corrective is clear. We shall all have to be more personally involved in the social revolution that is sweeping across the country. Jobs, education, housing, voting, public accommodations are all subjects of Christian concern. Churches that say and do nothing about them have lost touch not only with the realities of the contemporary situation but with the social implications of the gospel of Christ.

What does this mean for Riverside? It is a call to each of us to examine our priorities, to test and evaluate all our activities, to put the **primary stress**, where Christ did, **on serving God in human relationships.** Riverside does not exist to perpetuate itself but to give itself. It fails its mission if it draws people within its walls and monopolizes their time, skills, and money for its institutional life. It is in the thick of the world that the work of a Christian church is to be done. It is in caring and serving, in responding to human need, in righting social wrongs that God is known.

> "Did not your father eat and drink
> and do justice and righteousness?
> Then it was well with him.
> He judged the cause of the poor and needy;
> then it was well.
> Is not this to know me?
> says the Lord." (Jer. 22:15-16 RSV)

I shall have more to say about these weighty matters in the course of the fall and winter. I return to the Riverside pulpit on Sunday, September 29, and on that day we begin the work of another church year. I pray that it may be for all of us a day of dedication and commitment to Christ and his church, and, through them, to the service of the nation and the world.

Yours very sincerely,[19]

[19] Used by Robert J. McCracken, minister, Riverside Church, New York, N.Y.

THANK-YOU TO RESIGNING STAFF MEMBER

Dear Lynn:

Now that you have felt led to relinquish your duties as director of our Training Union, I wanted to express to you my deepest appreciation for your wonderful service.

I shall ever recall with joy your faithful devotion and your earnest and effective effort in the realm of Training Union here at First Baptist.

Thank you so very much for all that you have done. If I did not know how heavy your schedule at the University is, it would be much more difficult for me to see you relinquish your task. But I know that you must have some time for your family and other matters.

Thanking you again and may the Lord continue to bless you and use you, I remain

Faithfully yours,[20]

LETTER TO A VOLUNTEER WORKER

THANK YOU and GOD BLESS YOU

You have been invited to participate in a most important phase of Christian churchmanship. You have accepted the invitation. We express our deepest appreciation for your spirit of willing service and Christian commitment. It is people like you that make it a real privilege to serve as a minister of First Methodist Church.

I want you to know that I stand ready to assist you in any and every way possible. I hope that you will ask questions as we move along in this program of stewardship visitation. I hope that this will be a learning experience in churchmanship for every one of us.

[20] Used by R. Paul Caudill, minister, First Baptist Church, Memphis, Tenn.

The theme of the visitation is found in II Tim. 2:15. J. B. Phillips translates the verse this way: "For yourself, concentrate on winning God's approval, on being a workman with nothing to be ashamed of, and who knows how to use the word of truth to the best advantage."

Let us "concentrate." Please accept, in advance, my sincere thanks for your willingness to serve Christ and his church. My prayer, daily, is that God will bless you and enrich your life through this experience.

Sincerely,[21]

THANK-YOU TO BOARD MEMBER

Dear Board Member:

If you are already participating in the "friendly visitation" of our Evangelism Crusade, please accept this note as simply "thank you" for the important and helpful job you are doing.

So far, only a small percentage of the Official Board has helped in this significant responsibility. Won't you please arrange your schedule so that you can be at the church next Monday night at 6:15 p.m. for supper, a brief period of instruction, and then about two hours of calling on persons all over the city? These are persons for whom Travis Park Methodist Church is privileged, in the name of Christ, to be responsible.

Our response has been unusually fine, but in order to accomplish our goal, we must have more visitors. I shall be most grateful to you for your cooperation and assistance.

Sincerely,[22]

[21] Used by Robert A. Uphoff, minister, First Methodist Church, Seattle, Wash.
[22] Used by J. Walter Browers, minister, Travis Park Methodist Church, San Antonio, Tex.

CONGRATULATIONS TO GRADUATE

Dear Sally:

If I could arrange it, I would have the bells rung in the church tower for you next Sunday. Why? Because this month you complete an important section of your education. To finish a high school course in these days is of greater importance than ever before and it's harder, too!

I send you my heartiest congratulations. You also have my best wishes for your future.

Sincerely,[23]

ACKNOWLEDGMENT OF GIFT

Dear Mr. Poplinger:

This is a sincere "thank you"—from myself, four teachers, and thirty-seven youngsters—for the gift of the two-ton air conditioning unit which you gave for the room used by the junior department in the educational building.

On behalf of the church and the Board of Education, I want to thank you most sincerely for your gift. You can be assured that the unit will keep the room temperature most comfortable on the warmest summer day.

And thanks to you we can do something this summer we have always wanted to do: sponsor an afternoon Story Hour once a week.

I can assure you that my gratitude for your gift is shared by all of us.

Cordially yours,

[23] Used by David A. MacLennan, minister, Brick Presbyterian Church, Rochester, N.Y.

"GET WELL" NOTE TO MEMBER

Dear Mrs. Milne:

It is indeed good news to learn that you have now returned home from your stay in the hospital. I am so sorry I did not have an opportunity to visit you while you were there, but my associate, the Reverend George Root, has kept me informed as to your recovery progress.

I know what a joy it must be to be at home again amid familiar surroundings, and this will certainly add to your recovery power. Do take care of yourself and be sure of our continued concern and prayers.

With kindest good wishes and personal regards.

Cordially yours, [24]

CHRISTMAS GREETING TO SHUT-INS

Dear Prayer Partner and Friend:

There is no question in anyone's mind but that Christmas is the happiest time of the whole year. In spite of all of the commercial distractions, the Christian's heart rejoices in the wonderful fact that "Christ the Savior is born!"

You will accept from all of the staff and from the official family of our church the warmest, heartiest, and most sincere wishes for a Christ-centered, God-honoring Christmas. Added to all of this is our prayer that together the smiles and tears of 1964 will draw us closer to one another and together, closer to Christ.

Let me say again that if we can be of service to any of you in any way at any time, you will not hesitate to let us know. I remain

Yours in the Christ of Christmas, [25]

[24] Used by Kenneth A. Carlson, minister, First Methodist Church, Glendale, Calif.
[25] Used by W. C. Hultgren, pastor, First Baptist Church, Tulsa, Okla. (Sent as an enclosure with the *Ideal Magazine*.)

One final story: One day an elderly grandmother showed me a faded letter kept in her Bible. It was a brief congratulatory note written by her pastor in 1907. He thanked her for the splendid work she had done as teacher of a Sunday school class. Did she appreciate it? Only one who has seen the sparkle in her eyes as she reads and rereads it can realize how much. How wise and understanding her pastor was!

Now that we've considered some of the ways in which letters can keep you in touch with your members and co-workers, is there one thought, more than any other, that should be driven home? Yes. It's just this: Start today—right now—and watch for the many opportunities of using friendly letters in reaching countless persons in your congregation. And you'll probably agree with a Texas pastor who said, "I certainly believe in personal contacts, but I've discovered that a friendly letter is often better. Nothing equals the power of letters in building good will in my parish."

15

INCREASING
stewardship by mail

As a minister you are concerned with ways of arousing your members to greater realization of their responsibilities as Christian stewards. At all times you attempt to show how financial support is an investment in souls, a way of bringing Christ and heaven to men, a method of giving that lasts through all eternity.

Whatever method you use (and there are many), it must contribute to the conversion of the church to stewardship. You try to convince your members, in the words of Ralph W. Sockman, that "the test of a man is not how much money he makes, but how much he makes with his money."

Modern tithing—a twentieth-century adaptation of the ancient biblical principle of returning one tenth to the Lord—has kindled a revolution which is transforming American Protestant churches both spiritually and physically.

Several major denominations have launched tithing campaigns, with amazing results. Contributions in many congregations have doubled or tripled. Hundreds of new church buildings have been erected, and the support of missions, domestic and foreign, has been record-breaking. Most important, Leland Stowe reports in *Christian Herald*, "Individuals as well as congregations are discovering that the age-old Christian precept can bring them unexpected joys and rewards."

Obviously as minister you help in outlining the steps in a carefully planned stewardship campaign—a survey, conferences and special meetings with leaders, assignment of workers, choice of appeals, proper publicity, effective literature—but you often overlook one vital factor. That is the work which effective letters can perform in stressing the significance of investing money in Christ's cause.

Now this is more than just "sending out a few letters." You and your helpers should decide definitely upon information and appeals which are likely to produce the best results.

Here are some techniques which have proved effective: (a) Outline clearly beforehand your strategy. (b) Each letter (even in a series of five) should be complete in itself (good beginning, sound message, action close). (c) If more than one letter is used, be certain that follow-up messages have a refreshing and different appeal and at the same time repeat certain points that have been selected as keynotes of the campaign. (d) See that each stewardship letter has pull, a quality that gets a "yes" response. (e) Remember that several letters are required when something new is being introduced or when a sustained effort must be made because of the magnitude of the task. On some occasions, of course, an emergency arises and the time factor limits the mailing to one letter.

Many stewardship letters fail to produce the desired action for one basic reason. Too many ministers "sit down to write letters" without planning and preparation. Their ideas show it. Appeals are written as they occur to the writer. Thoughts are disjointed. The letters lack direction. As a result readers do not respond.

Before writing or dictating a stewardship letter you'll find it worthwhile to follow the procedure used by direct mail experts. Like this: (a) Define your objective. (b) Know what inducement, appeals, benefits, rewards you can offer. (c) Anticipate any reason the recipient might use in refusing to respond. (d) Pinpoint your prospect (his beliefs, moods, attitudes, feelings). (e) Devise a way to incite action *now*.

It's no easy task to write a series of unusually effective stewardship letters. But it can be done! Let's look at three letters which produced extremely gratifying results.

Dear Mrs. Rowland:

There are some conversations in life that we never forget. For me one of these was with Mr. Schlemmer, General Manager for AEC. In February of 1950 he was telling me about Richland and its needs. Then he said, "We want someone to come here as a minister of the church who will convince these people that they should unpack the last barrel of dishes."

There was history behind that statement, for he spoke concerning an insecure community. People did not know how long they would be there, hence were afraid to unpack the last barrel of dishes.

This insecurity is not limited to any one place or person. It is a part of the experience of all of us. In facing my own problems I have learned that there is a place that speaks with such power that I have been able to unpack that last barrel of fear. It is at the altar of God.

Each Sunday morning I enter the sanctuary with all my fears and phobias. I am spiritually and mentally run down. There is the hymn and the scripture—the sermon is for me too —God speaks to me. I go forth refreshed and renewed. It makes a difference when I worship regularly.

Join me at worship next Sunday morning and help me "unpack that last barrel" that has stood so long. See you in church—it makes a difference.

Sincerely,

Dear Mrs. Rowland:

Harry Wilson recently celebrated his ninety-fourth birthday. We had a lot of fun sharing it with him. We teased him, but

163

underneath all the gaiety was a deep love, affection, and respect for this man of God.

Mr. Wilson is the wealthiest man I know! He is not wealthy in terms of dollars but in terms of investments. He has invested his entire life in others. He has told countless numbers of boys and girls, men and women of the love of God through Jesus Christ. The result of his investments of time and talent are to be seen in persons in high political office, leading industrial corporations, and our educational institutions. Those in whom he has invested himself are building the homes for another generation of children. His life has made a difference.

You, too, may determine the future of our world. You, too, may make the investment of your time and talents in persons through the church of Jesus Christ. Will you join Harry and me in this thrilling and productive dedication? Pray about it and when your opportunity comes, say "Yes." It makes a difference.

Sincerely yours,

Dear Mrs. Rowland:

The other day I was chatting with one of the members of our church. She is one half of what our state has called a "mom and pop" business. She was telling me an interesting story.

You see, this year the decision was made to tithe the business and to give the tithe to our church. She was all excited about the experience. She said, "Why all of life is different. Business is better, our lives are happier, we have more than before. Besides, look at the wonderful things that are happening with the money that we are giving. I didn't know that tithing could make so much difference."

Mrs. Uphoff and I have been tithing for years and years. We, too, have known much peace, poise, and plenty as a result. We, too, have enjoyed the exciting thrill of being able to do unusual things for God.

164

Why don't you investigate and experiment in this area of life for yourself? I am sure that you will make discoveries that you never thought possible. It does make a difference.

At any rate, declare yourself for God and his church by making your pledge of treasure when our stewards contact you.

Sincerely, [1]

LINK YOUR APPEAL TO A CAUSE

In fund-raising procedures you will usually get better results when the appeal is linked to an event, a cause, a specific need. Even when you present the annual budget, it is well to break down the various items. Frequently an appeal letter is signed by the minister and also by chairman of the stewardship committee or some other person named to direct the campaign. Quite often the chairman of the finance committee writes a letter or several in a series. Here are a few examples of letters which performed their functions successfully.

Dear Brick Church friend:

"ANOTHER APPEAL FOR MONEY?"

Yes.

Didn't we just have one for the Emergency Fund for Freedom?

We did, on February 16.

Actually we Presbyterians only have three special offerings a year. Two are authorized by our General Assembly, and one by our own Presbytery. The first is the offering taken every

---

[1] These three letters, personally addressed by helpers and personally signed by Robert Uphoff, minister, First Methodist Church, Seattle, Wash., were sent to 8,100 members. Result: "immensely effective."

year in March for ONE GREAT HOUR OF SHARING. The second was the Emergency Fund to provide immediate financial help for those who are suffering in prison, or because of loss of employment, or who need money to continue their education for Christian service. The Presbytery appeal is for the Presbyterian Home of Rochester.

We need to realize that just because we receive what seem to us to be many appeals doesn't mean that we respond to them all!

Also, as Christians we must always remember that CHRISTIANITY IS CARING.

Because God showed us in Christ that he cares so much about us and about all his children, we too must care for those for whom Christ died.

I wish I could tell you of the babies, older children, men, and women who have literally been given a new lease on life through food, clothing, medicine, shelter provided last year through ONE GREAT HOUR OF SHARING.

We have so much—whether we get a bonus soon or not.

Make Sunday, March 8, ONE GREAT HOUR OF SHARING because we have many hours of CARING.

Sincerely and hopefully,

P.S. The enclosures are for you to examine—and use.[2]

Dear Mr. Wallace:

FIRST CHRISTIAN CHURCH PAYS OFF DEBT

Wouldn't it give you a thrill to see that headline in the "Duncan Daily Times"? Well, that headline will appear one of these days, because we lack only $785 on our debt.

[2] Used by David A. MacLennan, minister, Brick Presbyterian Church, Rochester, N.Y.

166

So what I am going to ask is—could you help us in ridding our church of this debt? You have always been more than generous in supporting the church, and I felt that you would be glad to make a "plus" pledge at this time.

With everyone sharing in the project we shall soon be able to clear our church of debt. Since we are so near our goal we cannot fail. We shall be expecting your reply soon.

Cordially yours, [3]

My dear Friends:

Sixteen years ago I wrote my first letter to this congregation asking each member to share in supporting the program and work of the church through the Every Member Canvass. The response through the years since then has been magnificent and a source of encouragement and gratitude. No congregation could have been more loyal.

Our church has grown both in numbers and in influence in a changing community and a changing world. We have come now to a day when we are confronted with a choice; slip back or move ahead. Our building program has been completed and we are comfortably and adequately housed. The work of the church is healthy and vigorous. The church is financially sound.

The challenge of the day, however, is great both here and overseas. There is unrest and confusion in the nation and a profound need for Jesus Christ as our standard for judgment in relation to contemporary issues. There are hunger and spiritual need in many lands where the church serves, and there is growing need for the ministry of the church in the inner city. The strains and anxieties which disturb individuals in our community call the church to a larger pastoral ministry and our youth are seeking guidance from the church.

[3] From *Successful Letters for Churches* by Stewart Harral (Nashville: Abingdon-Cokesbury, 1946). Used by permission. P. 65.

So, after many years as your minister, I join with your officers and leaders in asking your generous support when you make your pledge for 1964. Our budget of $285,000, a copy of which is enclosed, has been increased slightly and can be met if all of us share in dedicated giving. Consider your pledge prayerfully and make it the measure of your gratitude to God for the gifts of his grace beyond all you could ask or think.

The Every Member Canvass will begin on Sunday, November 3. Plan to be present at one of the two services that day and to welcome one of the men of the church who will visit your home that afternoon.

With every good wish, and may God bless and guide you.

Very sincerely, [4]

Good Friends:

WHO SUPPORTS THE CHURCH?

Obviously, it must be THE PEOPLE who care. And we all do care. When we were received into the church, we vowed to support the church by our PRAYERS, our PRESENCE, our GIFTS, and our SERVICE.

Although North Broadway has a larger membership than many churches, the support of every member is important. We do not have a few who carry the support load alone. SUCCESS-FULLY meeting the budget is each one's responsibility.

Our people are responding in fine fashion. Will you join them? Do today what you have been meaning to do—prayerfully consider this responsibility and RETURN your personalized SHARING CARD to the church TODAY. Another card is enclosed.

[4] Used by Harold B. Walker, minister, First Presbyterian Church, Evanston, Ill.

168

We will look for your reply in the mail. Thank you for your prompt attention.

Sincerely, [5]

STEWARDSHIP APPEAL TO NONMEMBERS

Dear Friends:

We want you to know how delighted we are to have the privilege of serving your family through our Christian Education Program. We hope you feel we are doing a good job in helping to undergird the character and spirit of your home.

We are about to observe our annual LOYALTY SUNDAY, April 19. This is the occasion when our people underwrite the budget operation of our church and make it possible for us to serve your family as we do.

While you are not officially a member of our church, we are grateful for your interest. Thus we are taking the liberty of inviting you to help sustain the Christian Education Program that is so important in a day when so many forces pull against character education.

To help children understand the importance of systematic support of the church, we appreciate it so much when parents encourage them to make a pledge to the church budget. They then receive a box of offering envelopes for weekly use.

A copy of our weekly "Outlook" is enclosed to acquaint you with the many dimensions of our interesting church program. And be sure we would be honored and delighted to have you with us on April 19. There is no pressure or embarrassment for anyone at the point of giving.

[5] Written by Robert B. Weaver, minister of administration, sent out over the signature of Harold G. Fike, Sr., finance campaign chairman at that time, and approved by Lance Webb, then minister, North Broadway Methodist Church, Columbus, Ohio.

Thanks so much for the trust you place in us. A warm welcome always awaits your family here.

Cordially, and with kindest good wishes, [6]

APPEAL FOR THANKSGIVING OFFERING

Dear Church Friends,

My scripture calendar yesterday told the story of a missionary physician in one of China's hospitals who cured a man of cataract. A few weeks later forty-eight blind men came to him from one of China's wilds each holding a rope held in the hand of the man who had been cured. He had led them in this way, walking in a chain 250 miles to the hospital.

Will you agree with me that there is no finer way of thanking the Lord for his manifold blessings to us than by telling others about him and leading them to accept his salvation? This is the truth behind our Annual Thanksgiving Missionary Offering. If God's bounty to us were only food, then we should thank him best by sharing food with the hungry. So with clothing or housing or medicine. God's highest gift to us, however, remains the gift of Jesus Christ and his gospel of forgiveness, of hope and of joy. This we MUST share with others if we would say "Thank-you" to him. This we CAN share as we have part in this blessed missionary stewardship, thereby touching an uncounted host.

> "Behold how many thousands still are lying
> Bound in the darksome prison-house of sin,
> With none to tell them of the Saviour's dying,
> Or of the life He died for them to win."

Why not plan now to use the attractive envelope enclosed, bringing it to our worship here on Thanksgiving morning at

[6] Used by Kenneth A. Carlson, minister, First Methodist Church, Glendale, Calif. (This letter is also signed by co-chairmen of Every Member Visitation Committee.)

11:00 a.m., or if you need to be absent from the city, bringing it on Sunday the twenty-fourth.

God bless you with the joy of sharing life's best.

Faithfully yours, [7]

"Praise the Lord; for the Lord is good."—Ps. 135:3

Dear Church Family:

Will you join a crusade? It is a crusade to keep alive the meaning of Thanksgiving Day, I would like each one of you to talk about it with everyone you meet. Each year the purpose of "purchase for Christmas" has been pushed farther back on the calendar. This year even dear old Halloween was entangled with tinsel on the counter next to children's costumes. You take it from there. Start talking. Start doing.

Thank God, in the church we can keep alive the spiritual fundamentals that gave birth to this nation under God. This is the significance of bringing in our pledges as our forefathers brought in the bounty of their harvest. A pledge is a concrete testimony of faith; you mean business with God, you dare to express your thanks by actually giving. It is a fact materialism is stepping up its pace all around us. The church must answer by stepping up the faith! What can you do? You can start now by stepping up your pledge. The crusade must be won!

Your pastor,

P.S. This coming Sunday there will be Festival Thanksgiving Services at 9:30 and 11 o'clock, with the dedication of pledges upon the altar. Wednesday, Thanksgiving Eve, at 7:30 our traditional Family Communion Service will be held in the sanctuary.[8]

[7] Used by W. Theodore Taylor, minister, Central Baptist Church, New York, N.Y.

[8] Used by Randall C. Phillips, minister, Wilshire Methodist Church, Los Angeles, Calif.

SPECIAL EASTER OFFERING

"If ye then be risen with Christ, seek those things which are above."—Col. 3:1

Dear Friends:

Each year during the Lenten Season most of us experience a desire to search for a deeper fellowship with the "risen Lord." I have often wondered, "Are we missing Easter?" Maybe we are and don't know it! We all know that Easter is not just a date on the calendar. It is not just a time to go about in new clothes. Easter is a time of blessings from God and it is possible to miss many of these blessings.

Missing blessings does not mean that God is going to pass us by. The Father who gave us the promise of immortality through the Easter message is always more willing to grant us his blessings than we are ready to receive them. This truth is self-evident in the sacrificial gift of his Son so that all men might become his sons.

If we miss Easter, then, it will be our own fault. We might say our own default. The blessings of Easter or the Christian life are given to the seekers—to those who desire the heavenly gifts.

As we prepare for Easter we recall the great message of promise that is to all who have stood by the open grave. Loved ones and friends have been called from our sides. Out of our loneliness for them we find in this Holy Day the affirmation that there is joy in the household of God.

Jesus once asked a searching question: "What does it profit a man if he gains the whole world, and loses his soul?" He was talking about personal choices which determine destinies. A person loses his own soul through his own wrong choices or through neglect or his inattention to the things of the spirit and not through any disinterest on the part of God, for he constantly desires us to come to him.

Your choices as to how you will spend Holy Week will

have much to do with the blessings you receive. Your church will provide several services of worship for you and your friends. Maundy Thursday will close with a service of silent communion and Good Friday will close with a program of worship through music. Then on Easter Sunday every child of God should be in his House of Prayer.

God's blessings will be awaiting you. Will you come and tarry a few moments with him?

Sincerely,

P.S. For your convenience I am enclosing a sacrificial Easter offering envelope. All of this offering will go for the work of Christ's church around the world.[9]

ANNUAL GIFT TO THE METHODIST HOME

Dear Members of First Methodist:

There are many ways to express greetings and wishes at this season, but I know of no better way than to say that we hope the Spirit of the One who came at Bethlehem will find a welcome and abiding place in your heart not only during the Holiday Season but through all the days to come.

We will celebarte his coming in our services this Sunday and in our Midnight Service on Christmas Eve. The presentation of the dramatic opera, "Amahl and the Night Visitors," Sunday at 7 p.m. will provide one of the great experiences of the season.

One Christmas tradition at First Methodist is the visit by children from our Methodist Home at Waco. Several of them will be present in both morning services and will make brief visits to many of the church school classes.

These will be joined by the entire Radio Choir from the Home to bring us a special program at the Supper-Group Time in the main dining room Sunday evening at 5:30.

[9] Used by J. Clifton Sprouls, while serving as minister of Linwood Methodist Church, Oklahoma City, Okla.

On Sunday we will also make our annual gift to the Home. We make it at Christmas, but it is for the support of those four hundred children who belong to us in a special way. It means life and love and hope for them.

I am enclosing a Christmas envelope which you may wish to use. Bring it to any one of the services on Sunday or to your church school class. If you are unable to be present, you may mail it to me at the church and I will see that it is included.

Sincerely,

P.S. The Christmas Eve Midnight Service begins at 11 p.m.—in the light of hundreds of candles.[10]

THE REWARDS OF TITHING

Dear Friend:

What is the reaction of people who tithe?

Not long ago I asked this question in a sermon and the answers came from some tithing families in our church. Never have I encountered persons more eager to communicate their experiences.

Let's listen to their comments:

"For the first time in our life, we learned how to budget our income."

"If you tithe you don't worry about being pressured. You know what you are giving is right. You give until you feel good about it."

"The real fun in being a 'rich man.' We now give $50 where $5 was 'all we could afford' before."

"It automatically brings the church into the center of our home."

[10] Used by Robert E. Goodrich, Jr., pastor, First Methodist Church, Dallas, Tex.

174

"Tithing not only takes faith but it strengthens faith—in life, in others, in one's self."

"Our nine tenths goes farther since we have started paying our one tenth to God."

"Tithing has brought us joy and peace, but best of all, it keeps us close to God."

As you read those testimonials, remember that they were not reprinted from a booklet. Nor a pamphlet. They were all offered voluntarily by your fellow church members.

Tithing, you see, is based on this principle: We believe that life is God's, that he made it, calls its end in his own time, and that life's secret meaning is to acknowledge our indebtedness and live in daily gratitude for his goodness.

Remember the words of Mal. 3:10: "Bring ye all the tithes into the storehouse, that there may be meat in mine house, and prove me now herewith, saith the Lord of hosts, if I will not open you the windows of heaven, and pour you out a blessing, that there shall not be room enough to receive it."

Accept his challenge and see what happens!

The Lord bless and keep you.

Your minister,

Dear Member:

"For God so loved the world, that he gave his only begotten Son." Does your knowledge of that fact ever lead you to ask, "What can I do for him?"

The apostle Paul answers our question in the following words: "Upon the first day of the week let every one of you lay by him in store, as God hath prospered him." (I Cor. 16:2.)

These verses from the Bible quoted above suggest clear and definite principles for the support of God's work:

1. Our giving to God must express sincere gratitude to him for what he has done for us.

175

2. Our gifts to God should be the first thing to come out of our incomes, not the last. ("Upon the first day of the week let every one of you lay by him in store.")

3. Our giving to God should be in proportion to the extent he has blessed us. ("As God hath prospered him.")

Tithing, or giving 10 per cent of our income, is taught in the Bible. Many of you have found joy in tithing. Some of you have not yet tried it. We hope that many of you will decide to give to God a tenth of your income in the coming year. But whatever you may decide, we encourage you to follow the practice of giving a definite percentage of your income as an offering to God.

Many Christians have wondered what constitutes a Christian standard for giving to God. We feel proportionate giving provides that standard. Consider a weekly pledge equal to one hour or more of your weekly wage.

On November 5, during the morning worship service, you will be given an opportunity to pledge a definite proportion of your income to God as an offering of gratitude to him.

We suggest you pray about it, then come on November 5 and offer God your best.

Sincerely, [11]

REMINDER LETTER OF INCOME TAX REGULATION

Dear Friend of St. Luke's:

Why not save some money on your current income tax bill? Many individuals and businesses give much thought to this subject at the close of the calendar year.

[11] Used by Walter R. Hobkirk, minister, Park Presbyterian Church, Newark, N.Y. (Signed by chairman of stewardship committee and chairman of canvass committee).

With the thought that the following might have been overlooked by some, we write this letter as a "reminder" that:

"Under current Income Tax Regulations (I.R.C. #170) it is possible to make deductions for contributions made to churches . . . up to 30% of their adjusted gross income (net business income)." If a contribution is made in property (stocks, bonds, real estate), the value of the property, not its cost, is the measure of the contribution for purposes of the deduction (Re. 1.170-1 (c). Any unrealized increase in value is not income subject to tax."

If you render your report on a calendar year basis, it is most important that your checks for contributions clear through the bank before December 31. Why not do it now?

CAN YOU THINK OF A BETTER WAY OR A BETTER PLACE. . . to make a substantial gift than to St. Luke's Methodist Church? This is a splendid way to help this worthy institution to continue its great work financially unhampered, and also to help you reduce your income taxes.

Sincerely,

THE FINANCE COMMISSION [12]

THANK-YOU BUILDS GOOD WILL

Too often the person who attends to his obligations promptly is forgotten in the rush of reminding those who are slow in paying their pledges. It takes only a few minutes to let a faithful member know that you appreciate his loyalty and cooperation, and such thoughtfulness is sure to build good will for your church. Write more brief "thank-you" notes to persons in recognition of their dependability as stewards. Note the following:

[12] Used by W. McFerrin Stowe, while serving as minister of St. Luke's Methodist Church, Oklahoma City, Okla.

Dear Mr. Bostwick:

In the busy life of our church sometimes we forget to say "thank you" to those who are faithful and loyal.

So I'd like to convey our thanks to you for the prompt manner in which your monthly pledges are always paid. Such a devotion marks you as one of our most loyal members.

It is my prayer that as you are sharing that which you have been entrusted that you will find the joy which comes only to him who knows the true meaning of Christian stewardship.

Sincerely yours,

Dear Mrs. Bartley:

Accept our thanks for the pledge which you have made to Forest Hills Presbyterian Church for the coming year.

Because of many new challenges and problems, our church must be kept strong in the critical year ahead. Your generous support is appreciated now more than ever before.

So thank you again for helping our church in advancing the Kingdom.

May the love of God be very real to you.

Cordially yours,

Dear Ralph:

We wish to thank you for your interest in our church as manifested by your gift to the "Let's Finish It Now" Building Fund Campaign.

It is the loyal sustained enthusiasm of every member, as expressed in this campaign, that makes our church a force in the community. We are confident that we will be even more effective because of our laboring together in this common cause.

178

May God continue to bless you richly for assuming as your responsibility a part in this program. We move forward in faith and gratitude.

Gratefully yours,

Pastor

So that we may have our records accurate, will you please check the information below regarding your pledge. If there is any error, please notify the church office.

PLEDGE _____

PAID WITH PLEDGE_____

GIFT _____[13]

In writing a stewardship letter, do these things:

1. Give the reader all the facts he will need in order to take the action you desire.
2. Motivate him as an individual to respond in the desired way.
3. Avoid the "this is just another appeal" but instead use a friendly, enthusiastic, persuasive tone.
4. Seek unusual ways of attracting attention and building conviction.
5. Show the spiritual dividends of stewardship.
6. End your letter on a constructive note, compactly presented.

Write enough letters like that and your people will respond heartily and joyously as they live their faith through stewardship.

---

[13] Used by W. McFerrin Stowe, while serving as pastor of St. Luke's Methodist Church, Oklahoma City, Okla.

16

TESTED
messages for many occasions

You've read fifteen chapters to see examples of effective letters and also to discover some of the ingredients which make a letter outstanding. By now you've probably spotted these basic elements:

1. The planned letter is always better than the canned letter. Only as you know the reader as an individual with his hopes, his fears, his human attributes can you gear your message to him.

2. Letter writing is the art of communication. But before you communicate you must commune—with people, with God, with the world around you, with yourself.

3. To write letters that get results, you must tap the brain and tug at heartstrings. And—you must have faith in what you are saying.

4. Be different. Be fresh and sparkling. But, above all, be sincere.

5. The best letter doesn't spring from the typewriter; it springs from the heart.

In short, it's the common touch in letters that give them power. You'll become a good letter writer as you develop what John Kelman called "the sympathy of the open-hearted." He said, "You will reach a truer knowledge of men by loving them and keeping your heart open to them than by studying their ways for a lifetime."

Now that we have considered the vital elements of church letters and have seen a number of specimen examples, let us examine some special types of tested letters that have been successfully used by pastors. Few of the letters are perfect—indeed, most of the authors will agree that the messages could be improved.

Letters appearing in this chapter deal with a wide variety of church situations. Some were used in mass mailings. They include welcome notes, notes of appreciation, seasonal greetings, and letters for other occasions. Obviously, like other letters in this book, there is some difference in their quality, but interestingly enough, each one performed its mission.

All of them show a wide variety of approaches to a church's public relations problems. But all of them have one very important element in common—they got results! Each one proved its effectiveness by building good will, understanding, and support; and equally important, each one extended the ministry of its church.

LETTERS TO NEW MEMBERS

Dear Mr. Tindall:

Let me tell you again how very happy I was to receive you as a new member of First Christian Church last Sunday.

During the next several weeks you will receive letters from the other ministers and leaders of the church. I encourage you to read their letters carefully and follow their suggestions. Their purpose is to help you derive as much spiritual joy from your church membership as possible.

Please remember that the church is the "body of Jesus Christ" seeking to do his work today. Its primary purpose is not to serve you or have you serve it, but that all of us, working in common faith and having the spirit of love, might serve Jesus Christ and his cause and so glorify God.

181

How much you do in the church, in terms of activity, will depend upon your training, time available, and talent; but by all means there are three things we all ought to do as active church members: (1) Attend the worship services regularly and support its work. (2) Witness to our Christian faith every day where we live and work. (3) Read our Bibles and pray daily.

My prayer is that you will grow in grace and serve God effectively through your church.

Yours in Christ, [1]

Dear Mr. and Mrs. Ambrister:

Welcome to Southern Hills Christian Church! We are happy and proud to have you as new members and we hope that you will receive spiritual strength as you become a part of our fellowship.

"Sunday at Southern Hills makes a difference," one of our members said recently. And we hope that the hymns of the church, the reading of the Bible, and the sermons will give all of us a new lift in our lives.

Let's try to be in God's house every Sunday. More than that, invite your friends to join us. Only as we become witnesses do we find the true joy of membership.

Sunday morning sermon: "The Imperatives of Life."

Most cordially yours,

WELCOME TO YOUNG PERSON

Dear Mike:

I want to welcome you into the fellowship of Central Christian Church. I feel that you have made a very fine decision in

[1] Used by Alfred E. Ellis, minister, First Christian Church, Houston, Tex. (first letter of a series of four).

becoming a part of one of the finest congregations in Indianapolis.

You know, of course, that the church becomes more meaningful to you as you become more involved in it. I will be looking for you every Sunday and hope that you will come to me some day and say, "What can I do to help the church?"

I want to be your friend as well as your minister. Call on me any time. Please know that I want to be of help to you in every way possible.

Very sincerely yours, [2]

LETTER TO PROSPECTIVE MEMBER

Dear Mrs. Hankins:

For seventy-five years St. Luke's has stood as a landmark in Oklahoma City, representing Christ and calling people to prayer and to service. Across these years it has been known for the wonderful people who made up its membership.

On this seventy-fifth Anniversary I want to invite you to become one of this fine group. We must do for our children what our parents have done for us. I know you believe in the church and understand how important it is for us to keep it strong and vital.

You are welcome to unite with St. Luke's at the close of any service, but if you have not by February 2, I am going to ask two of our members to come by to see you that week to answer any questions you have and to invite you in person to become one of us.

May God bless you and guide you in this important decision.

Cordially yours, [3]

[2] Used by Myron C. Cole, while serving as pastor of Central Christian Church, Indianapolis, Ind.

[3] Used by W. McFerrin Stowe, while serving as minister of St. Luke's Methodist Church, Oklahoma City, Okla.

NOTE TO LOYAL MEMBERS

Dear Hazel and Joe,

As I looked out over the congregation Sunday morning and saw you both in your accustomed place, I felt that I wanted to write and tell you how good it is always to see you at church.

You who have been faithful to the Lord and to his church through the years always bring joy to my heart.

With love and all good wishes for the days ahead, I remain

Faithfully, [4]

TRACE LETTER TO MEMBERS WHO HAVE DROPPED OUT

Dear Friends:

Memorial Drive Church is always interested in what happens to people. Although we have had tremendous growth in a short time, there are some people who seem somehow to stay with you, and this is how it is between you and us.

We appreciate your past attendance at our worship services and we trust that you have now located a church home. Our Evangelism Prayer Chain is made up of a group of sincere Christians who pray daily for our visitors. They have prayed for you and this may be one of the reasons why names become "people" rather than just names.

If you have joined another church, will you please phone our church office (SU2-1710) and let us know. We always rejoice whenever anyone in this rapidly growing section finds a spiritual home.

Meanwhile, if there is anything we can do for you at any time, please do call on us.

[4] Used by R. Paul Caudill, pastor, First Baptist Church, Memphis, Tenn.

May the love of the Lord be very real to you for every need.

Sincerely, [5]

LETTER TO THOSE MISSED IN HOME CALLS

Dear Friends:

Thank you for attending our worship services recently. We regret that our attempts to contact you either by phone or by visit to your house have not been successful. But we do want you to know we are grateful for your interest and hope you will visit us again.

Memorial Drive Church has had tremendous growth in its short history, but we are still very much interested in every person who comes to worship with us. Next time you are in church, if it is possible, please come by the main door after services and introduce yourself.

Meanwhile, if there is anything we can do for you in any way, please phone us. (SU 2-1710)

May the love of the Lord be very real to you.

Sincerely, [6]

LETTER TO VISITOR FROM ANOTHER LOCAL CHURCH

Dear Mrs. Cooper:

Thank you for telling us you worshiped with us last Sunday. It inspires us to know that fellow Christians from other churches worship with us from time to time.

[5] Used by Charlie W. Shedd and Jim Brock, ministers, Memorial Drive Presbyterian Church, Houston, Tex.
[6] Used by Charlie W. Shedd and Jim Brock, ministers, Memorial Drive Presbyterian Church, Houston, Tex.

If ever we may be of service to you, please call on us.

God bless you richly,

Sincerely yours, [7]

Dear Mr. Maloy:

I express my joy and appreciation to you for your presence in our worship service last Sunday. Christian worship is always enriched when it is shared with friends.

I pray that you felt spiritually at home in our church and that the service of Christian worship was a meaningful experience for you.

You may already have a happy church home in Houston. If so, we certainly wouldn't want you to neglect it, but if the opportunity arises again, we would welcome you as a visiting Christian friend.

If you are not a member of a church in Houston, we invite you to worship with us regularly; and, if you are interested, I would be most happy to talk with you, at your convenience, about your church membership.

If at any time I can serve you as pastor, please feel free to call upon me.

Most sincerely, [8]

LETTER TO VISITOR FROM OUT OF TOWN

Dear Mrs. McCann:

Your presence with us in morning worship in Brick Church last Sunday brought us joy.

[7] Used by David A. MacLennan, minister, Brick Presbyterian Church, Rochester, N.Y.

[8] Used by Alfred E. Ellis, minister, First Christian Church, Houston, Tex.

186

On your future visits to Rochester we want you to feel that our church is your church home away from home.

God bless you richly,

Sincerely yours, [9]

LETTER TO NEW BABY

Dear Pam:

So you have finally arrived in this big world! We are so happy that you have come to take your place in that grand Ersted family with Ralph and Lester. They have planned with great anticipation your coming, and you are fortunate, indeed, to have such a fine Christian home!

I covet for you the experience you will have under the influence of Christian parents. During the early years they will train you up in the way that you should go, and as you come to that period of adolescence which is so important, you will have already built a foundation for your life which will prove most helpful. The years ahead will be interesting and happy ones.

The church will hold an important place in your life, and I want you to remember through all of your life that in the teachings of Jesus we find the only bases for complete living. I pray God's richest blessing on you as you grow in wisdom and stature. May the days of your years be fruitful ones in service and in love for your family, your nation, and your Father God.

Very sincerely,

Your first pastor [10]

[9] Used by David A. MacLennan, minister, Brick Presbyterian Church, Rochester, N.Y.
[10] Used by Myron C. Cole, pastor, Hollywood-Beverly Christian Church, Hollywood, Calif.

REGULATIONS OF BABY NURSERY

Dear Friends:

So many members have asked about our baby nursery that we would like to give you the regulations governing it. Here they are:

Our baby nursery will be available during both church services, for babies THREE MONTHS TO ONE YEAR ONLY. TRAINED NURSES will be in charge.

PLEASE MAKE RESERVATIONS through the office BEFORE SATURDAY OF EACH WEEK. Our limit is eighteen babies. If you decide to cancel your reservation, please call the office immediately.

Mothers should bring:

1. Baby's formula, labeled, with written instruction.
2. One blanket.
3. Diapers and a moisture-proof bag.
4. A rattle or plaything for the older baby who sits up in the crib.

Health note: No baby should be brought who has been exposed to a contagious disease, who is ailing, or who has a cold.

IF FURTHER INFORMATION is desired, please call the church office—PE 4-8765.[11]

BIRTHDAY LETTER TO A CHILD (7 TO 10)

Dear Betty:

I hear you are celebrating a really great day: your birthday!

Here's a little prayer you could say on your birthday:

[11] Used by Hennepin Avenue Methodist Church, Minneapolis, Minn. From "Nursery Regulations," by Elizabeth W. Sudlow, *Church Business*, June, 1957, and reprinted by special permission from the Duplex Envelope Company, Richmond, Va.

"Dear Lord, thank you for giving me the wonderful gift of life, and for my home and family, my friends, and church and school. Help me to use my life rightly and to grow braver, kinder, wiser, year by year. Grant me your strength to help all those around me, and try to make them happy. Be with me step by step by step all through this new year, and keep me safe to the end. For your Love's sake. Amen."

Love from

Your friend and minister, [12]

LETTER TO CHILD ON DAY OF BAPTISM (TO BE OPENED ON HIS OR HER TWELFTH BIRTHDAY)

December 3, 1964

Dear Gwendolyn:

On this beautiful Sunday morning your father and mother stood before the congregation as they dedicated you to the Lord. As I took you from your father's arms, it was my great privilege to baptize you.

Your parents, in this way, dedicated you to God and themselves to rear you in the Christian way of life and to aid the Holy Spirit to bring you to a decision for Jesus Christ. All these years the church has been joining in prayer with them that you would honor the Lord in your life.

I hope that by the time you read this you will already be a member of the church. By now you are already making many decisions for yourself.

Your deciding to honor Christ in your life and to follow him

[12] Used by David A. MacLennan, pastor, Brick Presbyterian Church, Rochester, N.Y.

by being a Christian in the home and at school, at your work and at your play, will be the best happiness you can give to them and to yourself.

My prayer is that God will bless you as you grow into womanhood and that you will remember the vows which your parents took this day as they acknowledged their need for God in their lives and in yours.

Sincerely, [13]

LETTER TO ACOLYTES

Dear Richard:

You have been chosen to be an acolyte in our morning worship service. This is a great honor. You will be helping to bring the people closer to God. You will be helping to make the service more beautiful and meaningful. You will be helping our pastor as he leads the congregation in real worship.

Here are some points for you to read over with your parents and try to observe, as you fulfill this office:

1. Be present in the robing room at 10:45. Put on your vestments quietly. Hang your suit coat up. Go quietly to your station at the side of the sanctuary. Do everything slowly and reverently, even before the service begins. The candles should be lighted promptly at the stroke of 11:00.

2. On your face should be an expression of peace and calm at all times. Your chin should be raised. Your eyes should be high. Your body should be straight. Your steps need to be firm and not too short.

3. As you proceed down the aisle, watch your partner out

[13] This letter, written to the child on the day of his or her baptism, is given to the parents and is not to be opened until the child's twelfth birthday. Used by John F. Anderson, minister, First Presbyterian Church, Orlando, Fla.

of the corner of your eye. Always do everything together. But DO NOT TURN YOUR HEAD.

4. When you have lighted the candles, pause a moment before turning, to make certain that they are both burning.

5. After you have taken your seat, and laid your lighters on the floor, SIT UP STRAIGHT. A person who is hunched over in his seat is not an inspiring thing for the audience to look at. Place your back firmly against the back of the seat, keep your head up, and pay very close attention to everything.

6. PARTICIPATE in every act of worship: the singing, the praying, the reading, and the listening to the choir. You are still serving as assistant to the minister. Just by the way you sit and the way you conduct yourself, you can still be a blessing to the many people in the sanctuary.

7. You will NEVER WHISPER. This is an absolute rule. You will not "grin" if something does not go right. Just be calm about everything.

8. At the close of the service, after the choir has left, and immediately after the benediction, you will go to the altar again, and extinguish the candles. You will do this with the same reverence and care that you used at the beginning of the service.

9. Be sure that your lighter is put away safely, and that your vestments are hung straight on the hangers, and the fasteners are closed.

10. Here is a good verse of scripture for you to make your motto during these weeks!

> "He who is faithful in a very little is faithful
> also in much."   —Luke 16:10 RSV

Your minister,[14]

[14] Used by Donald B. Strobe, minister, First Methodist Church, Eaton Rapids, Mich.

INVITATION TO BECOME A "PARISH SHEPHERD"

Dear Friend:

Please allow me to take a moment of your time to explain to you an exciting new plan for our church, in which you will be invited to participate.

It is called the "PARISH SHEPHERDS" plan, and a fellow church member will be calling upon you soon to explain this to you and to enlist your aid (if he has not already done so).

You have been chosen because of your dedication to the cause of Christ and his church, and because your church feels that you are the type of person whom we would like to have to represents your church as a "Parish Shepherd." For the coming year, we would like to have you (together with some fifty other "shepherds") take the following responsibility:

1. **Get to know** who the Methodists are in your immediate neighborhood. (Their names and addresses will be given to you; more than likely there will be from four to six families.)

2. **Be "spiritually responsible"** for these fellow church members. Pray daily for each of them. Get to know what their spiritual needs are. If they are not active in the church, we want to know **why.**

3. **Once or twice during the year, you will be asked to contact** these fellow church members to help us keep them informed and involved in the work of the church. This can be done by a personal visit or, even better, by inviting several couples into your home for a brief "coffee and conversation" some evening. (If I am free that evening, I would like to come also. So please invite me, if it is convenient.) We want to do a better job of "shepherding our flock." **We need your help!**

4. **When newcomers move into your neighborhood,** call on them, invite them to share in the fellowship of your church, get acquainted with them. Then let us know about them.

5. **Write out** on a sheet of paper the names and addresses of the few families for which you are personally responsible. Then, a couple of times a year (after you have personally contacted them) leave a copy of this list at the church office with your comments which might help us to know and serve each of these families better.

6. Now, **specifically, you will be asked to discuss the current church budget** with the families in your neighborhood, and to answer questions about the work of our church for the coming year. You will not be asked to ask for pledges.

I hope that you will accept this responsibility when you are asked, for in this way you will be rendering a vital service by helping me to be a better pastor. You will be, in reality, an "assistant shepherd." I will appreciate your affirmative reply, when asked.

Sincerely, in Christ's service, [15]

LETTER TO COUPLE SOON TO BE MARRIED

Dear Helen:

I am so delighted that you and R. F. will exchange your wedding vows in our church on Saturday. And I want to send along now this word of personal good wishes and congratulations as you are both about to begin your great adventure together.

It will be a very wonderful moment when you stand at the altar and exchange your vows and I trust it will be one you will cherish for the rest of your lives.

[15] Used by Donald B. Strobe, minister, First Methodist Church, Eaton Rapids, Mich.

Be sure my thoughts will be with you on your memorable day, and Mrs. Carlson and I would like to extend our congratulations and good wishes for many happy tomorrows.

Cordially, [16]

LETTER OF APPRECIATION TO SUNDAY SCHOOL TEACHER

My dear Mrs. Merriman:

The session at a recent meeting voted that a special letter of gratitude be sent to you for your service in the Calvary Presbyterian Sunday Church School. Our thanks to you should, however, not be understood as an impersonal, official action but rather should be taken for what it is, an attempt to convey our personal appreciation to you as a fellow worker in Christ's church and mission. Furthermore, we should like you to understand that the rotation in the Sunday church school staff does not in any way preclude your return to teaching in the future or your present involvement in any other kind of service.

Through not only teaching subject matter but by so identifying yourself with the faith that a vital and dynamic meaning is transmitted, you have performed a great service for Jesus Christ through his church. It is not for us to assess the great influence or the profound effectiveness of what you have done, but we do thank God for your devoted effort.

We look forward to a continued happy and useful relationship with you in the family of God to which we have all been called through faith in Jesus Christ. May the blessing of God be with you in all your life dedicated to his service.

Sincerely, [17]

[16] Used by Kenneth A. Carlson, minister, First Methodist Church, Glendale, Calif.
[17] Used by Carl G. Howie, minister, Calvary Presbyterian Church, San Francisco, Calif.

194

GENERAL LETTER GIVING WORTH OF THE CHURCH

Dear Friends:

In this tangled, jangled generation people often ask, "What is the church? What is its role? What are its values?" Neil Wyrick gives us some of the answers in "I Am the Church":

"I am the church. I am high on a lofty hill. I am lovingly held in the soft curve of the green of the valley. I am caught on the brim of a deep blue lake. I am within sight of the shifting sands of the sea. My home is everywhere, and yet . . . my real true home is in the heart of man.

"I am the church. I am grey with the dust of a hundred years beneath my feet. I am white with the new look of completion. I am ageless in my stucco, my brick, my wooden frame.

"I am the church. I hold the lives of old and young. I make friends and see them marry, and see them die, and find new friends of faith to fill the gap. Glad songs ring through my rafters toward the sky. Prayers bow the heads of those within my walls. God's words echo through me with the wisdom of eternity.

"I am the church. A friend to those alone. An outstretched hand to those in pain. An ever present help in time of need.

"I am the church. I am not perfect. For though I represent a perfect God, my reins are held by imperfect men. But still my great steeples point to heaven. My crosses point to eternity. And the message preached to my people points to salvation. My efforts are not in vain; for sometimes one man enters my doors and a "new man" later leaves.

"I am the church. I am glad of my heritage. Humble before my responsibility. And with a great hope and love for all men."

Your minister,[18]

[18] From *Church Management*, October, 1958. Used by permission of the publisher.

So Easter Is Here Again

Almost twenty centuries ago the darkness of the world was shattered by an explosion more illuminating than the atomic bomb which fell on Hiroshima in Japan. In fact the atomic bomb split the sky in two, but by some sinister power it allowed a new darkness and dread to engulf our world. On the contrary, the explosion which pierced the darkness just before the dawn, on that first Easter, released a light that not only caused the guards about the tomb to stagger and fall as though paralyzed, but has compelled peoples in every century to fall upon their knees and cry out with Thomas, "My Lord and my God." The atomic bomb created tombs by the thousands. The quiet explosion of Easter morn opened all tombs. The bomb brought death; the Resurrection brought life. The bomb brought frightening destruction; the Resurrection brought joyous hope. The bomb opened a new "Era of Brinkmanship," where men test each others nerves. The Resurrection revealed the shoreline of a new era that brings God and man into a redemptive fellowship.

So Easter is here again.

You can ignore it, if you care to. You can say it is the same old stuff. You can mouth the pious phrases and get a momentary thrill. But doing any one of these things will leave you wandering in the same kind of spiritual darkness that sent the atomic bomb upon an Oriental city.

On the other hand, Resurrection can bring you the thrill of the dawn. It can impart to you the strange inner glow that manifested itself to the men on the Emmaus road. You can discover that sudden illumination which flooded the soul of doubting Thomas.

Easter A.D. 1964 is no different than Easter of A.D. 31. The Resurrection revealed Christ alive then, it reveals Christ alive now. Before the event there was sadness and disappointment then; even as there is uncertainty and fear today. Then the doors were locked against men; today, too often, the doors are locked against God. Why not make this Easter the time of Resurrection for our own lives? In A.D. 31, it worked for Peter and Thomas. Today it can and will work for you and me if we desire it.

Sincerely,[19]

CHRISTMAS LETTER TO CONGREGATION

Dear Friends:

Advent and Christmas are sacramental of life's highest glory to those who can see.

Have you ever stopped to wonder at the power the simple stories of the Nativity have on our minds? Classed by some as legends or fables, obviously not as accurate as a photograph would be, yet they are charged with a deep reality: God is revealed in them. God speaks his clearest word to us about our lives, about himself, about eternal values not in a palace of wealth or earthly success but in a stable. The glory of God shines in a baby, and the glory is shared by an ox and an ass and a few simple shepherds. Even the wise men who follow the star find God not in some complex mathematical equation describing cosmic reality but in a baby resting in a manger.

No matter how long we meditate on these simple stories, their truth is never exhausted. When we understand their meaning, we begin to see all our experiences in a glorious new light.

Then all life has meaning, for we see God in
    the last blush of the sunset's touch,
    the wonder of one who loves so much,
    the pure beauty of an infant's face,
    the glory of a simple act of grace,
    the grandeur of a family at prayer,
    the majesty of a parent's care,

[19] Used by Morgan Williams, minister, while at First Methodist Church, Chicago, Ill.

> the fragrance of the Christmas pine,
> the starry heaven's silver shine,
> the moonlight on fresh-fallen snow,
> the sacrifice of love we know,
> the power to think with him God's thoughts.
> These infinite blessings cannot be bought!
> Lo, heaven comes again to earth,
> And brings its blessings of rebirth!

In this day of complex confusions when we are lost in the profusion of demands, "things are in the saddle and ride mankind." We need to let the simplicity of Christmas bring us again to the values that never pass away. My prayerful suggestions to each of you during these days that may be for you either beautiful and holy or ugly and frustrating are:

1. Take **time** to **see** the deeper meanings behind the stories, carols, and rituals of Christmas. Else you will be "fed up" with them as childish foolishness and you will be just another Scrooge.

2. Take **heart** to **feel** the mystic Presence of him whose coming turns a stable into a King's chamber, and a sheep cote into a cathedral. Our souls are fed and lifted by worship and intelligent prayer.

3. Take **love** to **give** your gifts to the Highest by going beyond the swapping of earthly toys to the sharing of heavenly joys with those who know them not.

The accompanying brochure tells a thrilling story of what your gifts may do to let Christ come in Argentina, in India, and in our own Columbus town. Remember, only those who **see** follow the star; only those who **hear** listen to the angel's song; and only those who **love** will be born anew that holy day.

I speak for all your ministers and staff when I say, a blessed Christmas to you all!

Sincerely,[20]

[20] Used by Lance Webb, while serving as minister, North Broadway Methodist Church, Columbus, Ohio.

"KEEPING CHRISTMAS"

There is a better thing than the observance of Christmas day, and that is,

KEEPING CHRISTMAS.

Are you willing to forget what you have done for other people, and to remember what other people have done for you; to ignore what the world owes you, and to think what you owe the world; to put your rights in the background, and your duties in the middle distance, and your chances to do a little more than your duty in the foreground; to see that your fellow-men are just as real as you are, and try to look behind their faces to their hearts, hungry for joy; to own that probably the only reason for your existence is not what you are going to get out of life, but what you are going to give to life; to close your book of complaints against the management of the universe, and look around you for a place where you can sow a few seeds of happiness—are you willing to do these things even for a day?

THEN YOU CAN KEEP CHRISTMAS.

Are you willing to stoop down and consider the needs and the desires of little children; to remember the weakness and loneliness of people who are growing old; to stop asking how much your friends love you, and ask yourself whether you love them enough; to bear in mind the things that other people have to bear in their hearts; to try to understand what those who live in the same house with you really want, without waiting for them to tell you; to trim your lamp so that it will give more light and less smoke, and to carry it in front of you so that your shadow will fall behind you; to make a grave for your ugly thoughts, and a garden for your kindly thoughts, with the gates open—are you willing to do these things even for a day?

THEN YOU CAN KEEP CHRISTMAS.

Are you willing to believe that love is the strongest thing in the world—stronger than hate, stronger than evil, stronger than death—and that the blessed life which began in Bethlehem nineteen hundred years ago is the image and brightness of the Eternal Love?

THEN YOU CAN KEEP CHRISTMAS.

And if you keep it for a day, why not always?

—Henry van Dyke

SEASON'S GREETINGS from the Church Staff [21]

MOTHER'S DAY LETTER

Dear Friends:

As I look back to my childhood days, I find a most interesting memory among many others. My father held our mother, his comrade, in high regard. He would often help her in the house, and whenever possible he would ask her to come out with him when he was working in the yard. In other words he gave our mother a place of dignity, love, and appreciation. Hence, it is not very strange that the children in the family respected and loved their mother.

To me it seemed a bit strange to have a special day set aside for the honoring of mothers. We had been taught to honor our mother every day. She was in a unique fashion a queen on a throne. She worked hard and taught us how to work—not only taught us, but saw to it that we kept at it.

It does seem valuable to have a day set aside in which we seek to express directly and indirectly our appreciation for mother and motherhood. As a young man I still remember a phrase which was used for a mother's day sermon, "The Arresting Presence of Mother." As I recall it, the minister used this almost entirely as the spiritual influence of a mother long after she is dead and gone. I felt then and still do that such an approach has some value; however, there is a much deeper truth

[21] From *The Spirit of Christmas*. Used by Donald B. Strobe, pastor, First Methodist Church, Eaton Rapids, Mich.

as we sense the influence of one person on another. A mother literally shapes the destiny of her child. As the Eternal Creator breathed in man and he became a living soul, in some such fashion mothers breathe into their children the hopes and fears, the attitudes and reactions, the total feel toward life that will dominate them through the years.

Any mother who gives to her children a wholesome, sane, and unselfish attitude toward life and society has made a contribution toward human welfare, which can never be measured.

When we realize that today one out of every ten people has deep emotional disturbances, it gives us something to estimate how adequate or inadequate have been the mothers of yesterday. No woman can possibly fulfill her mission as a mother without a deep commitment to God, to life, and at the same time have a willingness to sacrifice for the welfare of her children and the society in which she lives.

Phillips Brooks said, "The world moves forward on the feet of little children." I would add that whatever progress is made depends very largely upon the quality of the lives of the mothers of the children.

Sincerely,[22]

SPECIAL LETTER TO PARENTS

How to Get the Most Out of Your Home

1. Be alert to use special occasions in the home as a time of worship. Anniversaries, birthdays, holidays, and religious festivals are appropriate times for special worship experiences.

2. We need to spend more times as families at home. Our living rooms have often become leaving rooms. Let us plan and schedule for time together as a family.

3. Let's participate more as families in the great occasions observed by our church—communion, Easter, church night

[22] Used by Morgan Williams, while minister at First Methodist Church, Chicago, Ill.

dinners, special musical programs, summer camps, and Christmas programs.

4. We can strengthen family by reading the Bible together. Little children can play some of the stories in the Bible.

5. As church families we should read and discuss religious literature in the home.

6. For goodness' sake, don't allow yourself to get into the thought patterns where the church represents religion and the home something else. So heavy is this truth that I can say to you, "If your child doesn't get religion in his home, he won't get it."

7. Always give blessings at the table—but don't expect the kids to do it every time. Have your children ever heard you pray?

8. Open your home to the young people of the church. It's easy. Have you ever entertained your child's Sunday school class and teacher at a party in your home?

9. Make the meal times an enriching religious experience for the whole family (rather than repeating all of the latest gossip and bad news in the headlines).

10. Share in stewardship as a family. Just as a child learns attitudes of worship from his parents, so he learns the values and joys of sharing his time, talents, possessions, and beliefs.

11. Plan for Christian symbolism in the home. The Bible, good religious pictures, or a cross will remind children that yours is a Christian home.

12. Remember these words from Deuteronomy: "And thou shalt love the Lord thy God with all thine heart, and with all thy soul, and with all thy might. And these words, which I command thee this day, shall be in thine heart; and thou shalt teach them diligently unto thy children, and shall talk of them when thou sittest in thine house, and when thou walkest by the way, and when thou liest down, and when thou risest up."

INDEX